PRAISE FOR *TRUST RULES*

"We all know that creating a great place to work is critical to a company's long-term success, but how do managers actually accomplish this? Bob Lee's book provides sixteen clear, concise principles and guidance on how to apply them to build employee trust in any industry or type of organization."

—Alex Edmans, professor of finance,
London Business School

"Here's the book every manager should read. Bob Lee highlights sixteen rules managers should follow to build trust within their teams and organizations. In very clear and straightforward language, Lee encapsulates lessons based on research from Great Place to Work's huge database of employee surveys and best management practices and his more than fifteen years of interviewing managers."

—Robert Levering, cofounder, Great Place to Work

"Bob Lee has written a book that is badly needed. A book which (at last) really helps managers at all levels to do their job well. Lee's book takes all the academic mumbo jumbo and consultant bullshit out of leadership and presents leadership as it should be—plain and simple human-to-human interaction. *Trust Rules* offers easy and actionable guidelines for every manager to act on. A big plus is its length: there's not a single sentence too much. It's easy and fun to read, so it's also ideal for the managers who don't usually read books. Bringing the concept of trust into the heart of leadership is a wise and well-grounded decision, because without trust, leaders have nothing."

—Panu Luukka, founder and corporate
culture designer, Leidenschaft

"*Trust Rules* provides succinct, smart, practical guidance on how to create a high-trust, high-performing workplace. Every manager should read this book and refer to it often."

—Michael Burchell, expert, organization
solutions, McKinsey & Company

"The goal of creating a great company culture can sometimes feel daunting. Bob Lee's *Trust Rules* breaks the process down into easy to understand management practices that can be applied on a daily basis to improve the work environment. It is a book that not only gives an immediate jolt of inspiration but also serves as a reference guide with practical ideas and reminders."

—Erin Moran, chief culture officer,
Union Square Hospitality Group

"*Trust Rules* works on so many levels. It's simple yet sharp, an easy, thoughtful read. Most important, it provides real context—and that's where it's different from other books. It's a great read for every level of manger because it acts as a powerful reminder for us to do the right things right."

—Garry McCabe, human resources director,
Kuehne + Nagel

"An informative and easy read. Being relatively new to the world of management, I recommend diving headfirst into this book. Everyone constructs their own management style—if you are in search of yours, you'll find inspiration and clear direction within these pages."

—Luke Taaffe, front office manager,
Clontarf Castle Hotel

"*Trust Rules* is a practical guide for managers at any stage of their career. In our ever-changing workplace it is inspiring to read a book that teaches managers how to lead in a way that embraces the enduring values that build and maintain extraordinary workplaces."

—Cheryl Naja, director of pro bono and
community service, Alston & Bird

"I love Bob's approach to leadership. *Trust Rules* is a breath of fresh air, a set of simple, pragmatic rules to govern the relationship between leaders and teams based on the principles of respect, kindness, decency, and positivity. A rare thing!"

—Colum Slevin, entertainment and technology executive

"Credit Bob Lee for creating one of the most insightful road maps for how to effectively build trust in the workplace and win the hearts and minds of employees. The sixteen rules presented in his book are a treasury of practical and valuable guiding principles that will nurture a more healthy, enjoyable, and productive work environment. *Trust Rules* is a compelling and useful book for anyone who wishes to become not just a good manager but an excellent manager who aims to build a great place to work and deliver exceptional business results. Trust rules!"

—Ramiro Garces, global HR consultant,
employee engagement expert and speaker

"Bob Lee generously shares the playbook on how to become a world-class manager. Full of insightful and actionable items leaders can start using today, *Trust Rules* provides all the tools necessary to manage today's dynamic and diverse workforce at the highest levels."

—Alex Chung, author of *Highest Success*

"This book is full of energy. You'll learn in simple terms what it takes to form relationships, build high trust, and create high-performance teams. Reading this book is 'one simple thing' you can do to immediately start improving your leadership skills."

—Colin Wallace, head of HR services, Europe, Sanofi

"*Trust Rules* highlights how important it is for managers to reflect on their own practices and be conscious of the impact these practices have on their teams. It's a good toolkit to remind us that, fundamentally, management is about treating people with respect and showing care."

—Caroline Texier, EMEA program manager, Dell EMC

"*Trust Rules* hits the mark in a simple, no-nonsense way—I loved it! Bob's book is for managers, leaders, and executives. Mostly, though, it's for people. People who understand that being good and decent are prerequisites for leading others. His rules fit with the Great Place to Work model like a tight glove, and they serve as critical reminders of the simple, though often forgotten principles of good leadership ."

—Hal Adler, CEO, Leadership Landing

TRUST RULES

TRUST RULES

**How the World's Best Managers
Create Great Places to Work**

BOB LEE

Published by Trust Lab Press, Dublin, Ireland
thetrustlab.com

Edited and Designed by Girl Friday Productions
www.girlfridayproductions.com

Interior Design: Paul Barrett
Cover Design: Paul Barrett

GREAT PLACE TO WORK is the registered trademark of Great Place to Work Institute, Inc.

The Trust Index Survey, the Culture Audit, and the Great Place to Work® Model are the copyrighted works of Great Place to Work Institute, Inc.

Paperback edition: 9780995737891
Deluxe paperback edition: 9780995737808
e-ISBN: 9780995737853

First Edition

Special discounts are available on quantity purchases by corporations, associations, and others. For details, please contact sales@thetrustlab.com

I was inspired to write this book by the many managers around the world who choose to treat people with respect, decency, and kindness. They make a positive difference in the lives of others and they make the world a better, nicer place.

If you're one of those managers, thank you. Keep it up.

TRUST
RULES

CONTENTS

INTRODUCTION

MANAGERS MATTER.

A manager makes the difference between whether an employee loves or hates their job. A bad manager can single-handedly ruin the workplace experience—regardless of how much effort senior leaders make to build a decent workplace culture. A good manager puts a team well on the way to an enjoyable workplace experience. But a *great* manager does even more.

A great manager can build a remarkable environment for their team even when most people would not regard the wider organization as a good place to work. They can ensure that their team is strong, loyal, and committed, even when surrounded by other managers whose teams are floundering and losing valuable employees faster than replacements can be recruited. Generally, employees don't leave an organization, they leave their managers. And when they stay, it's often their manager who keeps them there.

The telltale signs of a poorly managed team are easy to spot: More "they" than "we" when talking about their colleagues. Poor cooperation and little collaboration. Sarcasm. Eye rolls. One-sided "conversations." Below-par results, both individual and team. High stress. High absenteeism. High employee turnover. And most noticeable of all, a bad atmosphere.

The signs of a well-managed team are equally visible. Genuine conversations. Plenty of "us" and "we." Cooperation and collaboration. Laughter. People who plan to stick around. Happy people. And great results.

We know the kind of manager we want to be, and yet something strange happens to many of us when we're given the opportunity to manage. Make us responsible for others and we struggle to create the kind of workplaces that we would want for ourselves. We know the behaviors and attitudes that we value in the people who have managed us—those that make us feel good, valued, respected, and happy. Yet we often struggle to put this knowledge to work in how we deal with *our* employees.

To bridge this disconnect, many of the world's leading employers have, over the last thirty years, evolved a philosophy and a way of managing people for the changed reality of the knowledge economy. Their aim is to bring out the best in people, to engage their whole selves. They know that, without those people, they would have no business. It's logical, but not every organization gets it. Although most *say* that their people are their greatest asset, they manage them as if they were ancillary to their prospects of success—in other words, they are an afterthought. This is a major mistake and a missed opportunity because what sets the world's best employers apart from everyone else is the quality of the relationships in the workplace. And what single factor decides the quality of those relationships? Simply, the level of *trust* between managers and their employees.

Most of us have never stopped to think about the importance of building solid relationships with our employees. That's because most of us have never learned why it matters. Mainstream management thinking has failed to keep up. They don't teach trust in college. It doesn't feature in MBA programs. And it doesn't feature in most in-house training. That's a problem. We're taught how to *manage the resources* for which we are responsible—facilities, machinery, equipment, vehicles; we have learned how to *manage the people* who use those resources; and we know what we must achieve with those resources—production targets, sales budgets, service standards. But most of us have never been explicitly taught that the way to achieve these targets—and to achieve lasting success as a manager—is through building *trust* with each of our employees.

The Oxford Dictionary defines trust as "a firm belief" in a person's "reliability, truth, or ability." It's the key to great relationships between managers and employees, and those relationships are the foundation stone of the trust culture on which all great workplaces are built. As a manager, every word that you speak and every action that you take has the potential to affect trust, either positively or negatively.

Why this focus on trust? To understand that, we must go back to the 1980s and a book idea that proved to be the seed of a global workplace revolution.

TRUST AND THE GREAT WORKPLACE

In 1981, a New York editor offered two business journalists, Robert Levering and Milton Moskowitz, a challenging project: find the best companies to work for in America, figure out what makes them special, and write a book about it. Levering and Moskowitz spent the next two years traversing the United States visiting organizations that had reputations for being good employers, and they published their findings in their 1984 *New York Times* bestseller *The 100 Best Companies to Work for in America*. They had expected to find that these companies stood out because of a shared set of extraordinary employee benefits and programs, but what they discovered completely surprised them. Although they *did* find a wide range of generous and imaginative practices, they quickly realized that what made these workplaces *great* was something much more powerful than quirky perks and benefits: it was spirit.

"You could feel that spirit when you first walked through the door," Levering explains. "Often just by how the receptionist greeted you. Or how the employees interacted with each other in the hallways in such an open and friendly way . . . I learned that what was truly distinctive about the very best workplaces was the way in which employees and management got along with each other. In particular . . . I observed an extremely high level of trust between the management and employees. By contrast, really bad workplaces are characterized by the lack of trust."[1]

Levering realized that what created this spirit, what set these great workplaces apart from all others, was the quality of three interconnected relationships centered on each individual employee:

1. The relationship between the employees and their leaders, reflecting the level of *trust* between them.

2. The relationship between the employees, their jobs, and the organization, shown in the *pride* that they took in their work.

3. The relationships that employees enjoyed with one another, seen in the level of *camaraderie* in the workplace.[2]

Based on these insights, in 1991 Levering went on, with Amy Lyman, to found the Great Place to Work Institute, an organization dedicated to building and recognizing great places to work around the world. I joined them about ten years later. Our definition of a great workplace is unchanged since those early days, reflecting the timeless nature of human relationships. Simply put, a great place to work is one where you *trust* the people you work for, have *pride* in what you do, and *enjoy* the people you work with.

What we've learned over the years is that although you'll find pride and camaraderie in every high-trust team, you won't necessarily find high trust in every team that shows great pride and/or camaraderie. For example, you can feel proud of your personal contribution and that of your team, yet have little trust in your employer, making for a bad workplace. And it's common to find great unity in lousy workplaces—but it's a negative, often destructive, us-against-them type of togetherness, the type that you'd likely see among striking workers on a picket line!

Trust alone defines the quality of the workplace. Find low trust and you've found a bad workplace; find high trust and you've found a great one. And where you find high trust you will always find a great manager and a great place to work.

It's impossible for an employee to have a good all-around workplace experience unless they trust their manager. It's not a nice-to-have or an optional extra. Strong manager-employee relationships are the key factor in creating great workplaces and driving an organization's business performance, which explains why the world's best managers focus so much of their energies on building high-trust relationships with their teams.

But what's the big deal about great workplaces anyway?

HOW ORGANIZATIONS BENEFIT FROM BEING A GREAT PLACE TO WORK

The world's best workplaces are more successful than their peers, consistently outperforming them on every business metric that matters. All peer groups. Every metric. Extraordinary success. That's what makes them worth emulating.

For close to thirty years now, Great Place to Work has researched the various advantages that organizations that build high-trust workplaces enjoy, and each year *Fortune* magazine publishes our list of the 100 Best Companies to Work For. Annual studies of six thousand organizations representing more than ten million employees in eighty countries show that high-trust organizations attract and keep top talent, innovate more and better, give higher-quality service, and deliver stronger financial performance.

Strong financial performance is one advantage of high-trust organizations. Research shows that companies with high-trust cultures consistently generate superior returns for their investors. For example, independent investment firm FTSE Russell reports that the stock market returns of the publicly held high-trust companies recognized by Great Place to Work and *Fortune* over a seventeen-year period are nearly three times greater than the market average. A separate study found that a portfolio of India's Best Workplaces outperformed Indian stock market indexes by a factor of nearly four during the five years leading up to 2013.[3]

A four-year research project led by Alex Edmans of the London Business School into the *Fortune* 100

Best Companies to Work For proved conclusively that employee well-being precedes positive financial performance.[4] In other words, taking good care of employees *causes* good financial performance.

"The 100 Best Companies to Work for in America delivered stock returns that beat their peers by 2 to 3 percent per year over a 26-year period," said Edmans in a TEDx Talk on the topic. "Simply put: companies that treat their workers better do better. And this fundamentally changes the way that management should be thinking about their workers."[5]

Which brings the discussion neatly back to you as a manager! The evidence is clear—treat your team better and your team will achieve better results. Edmans's findings set you free to be the decent, caring manager that you want to be, and he is excited by what this means: "As managers, we can act responsibly without doing a calculation, without expecting anything in return, to do things for intrinsic and not instrumental value. And even though financial rewards were not the motive for acting ethically they typically manifest anyway."[6] In other words, do the right thing because it's the right thing to do, and the performance rewards will follow.

HOW MANAGERS BENEFIT IN A
HIGH-TRUST WORKPLACE

During our years of research at Great Place to Work, we've learned that, even in organizations that are not particularly strong workplaces, managers who build high-trust relationships with their employees and create positive workplace experiences for their teams get plenty in return. These managers point to several ways in which they are better able to do their work when they build trust with their employees:

- *Their teams can focus all their energy on achieving business objectives.* Their employees don't suffer the various distractions that are common in low-trust environments, such as internal politics, poor communication, or lack of clarity about goals.

- *They get the very best that each employee can offer.* When people feel they are working in an emotionally safe and secure environment—one that protects their mental health and well-being—they feel empowered to do their best work and they want to contribute to the best of their ability.

- *The team becomes more than the sum of its parts.* When they feel trusted and in turn trust each other, employees come to view their colleagues as more than just coworkers. They feel they belong to something bigger than themselves, and often use the term "team" or "family" to describe this idea. This sense that "we're all in this together" encourages employees to think about the greater good of people on their teams and the wider organization, instead of only looking out for their own individual interests.

HOW EMPLOYEES BENEFIT FROM HIGH-TRUST MANAGEMENT

Managers are not the only ones who derive benefits from high-trust relationships with their employees. Here are just some of the rewards your employees can enjoy from working in a great workplace:

- *Employees fit in well and they feel "at home."* Great workplaces enjoy great reputations and they attract many more job applications than their peers. They also understand the employee attitudes and values that best match the needs of the organization. So, great workplaces enjoy a triple advantage: they know what they are looking for; they get to search among a bigger pool of interested candidates; and they are expert at finding the right person for each job. The employee who makes it through the screening feels welcome, instantly at home, and ready to do great things.

- *Employees feel respected, valued, and cherished.* Having found the right people, great workplaces provide a caring environment that welcomes, engages, and keeps them. Supported by their managers, employees enjoy work-life balance, the freedom to take time off when necessary, and the knowledge that their unique contributions are recognized and appreciated.

- *Employees find meaning and enjoyment in their work.* In great workplaces, employees experience a creative and innovative work environment that allows them to make an impact on the company and, often, on the world around them. Employees find enjoyment and satisfaction in their work because they understand how what they do contributes to the overall goals of the team.

• *Employees work hard but suffer less stress.* Employees in great workplaces report greater control over how and when they do their work, and a strong sense that their managers understand and appreciate the pressure that they work under. Being in control means that employees can work hard, often under time constraints or other pressures, without feeling unduly stressed. Hard work and stress don't always have to go together. Great managers get that.

• *Employees have jobs that last.* Great workplaces are more financially successful and outperform their peers on a wide range of performance measures. Their greater financial strength coupled with strong brands and high levels of customer loyalty make these organizations more resilient in tough times than their competitors. High-trust organizations tend to emerge quicker and stronger from crisis than other businesses with less collaborative and respectful cultures, which gives their employees a degree of insulation from market shocks and consequential pay cuts or layoffs.

Everyone benefits from high-trust workplace relationships. Society. Investors and customers. Your organization, your employees, and you. So, how can you play a role? How can *you* become a great, high-trust manager?

FINDING THE TRUST RULES

I worked for more than fifteen years with executive and senior leaders in a wide variety of organizations around the world, sharing Great Place to Work's unique insights and ideas to help them develop their own great workplaces. I became intrigued by why, even in the very best workplaces, there were pockets of deep unhappiness— teams for whom the day-to-day workplace experience was very different from that of their colleagues elsewhere in the organization. I came to realize that programs driven from the top or by HR with the intention of improving the overall workplace culture count for little if the manager isn't strong. In short, if you have a bad manager, you will experience a bad workplace, regardless of your senior leaders' positive intentions.

So, I set out to understand exactly what it is that the best managers are doing right that other managers are doing wrong. I carefully studied feedback from almost two million employees in eighty countries around the world to better understand how great managers build trust, and to identify the manager attitudes and behaviors that have the greatest impact on how employees experience the workplace. I found that, except for some minor variations reflecting national cultural norms, the factors an employee considers when deciding whether or not to trust their boss are much the same the world over, regardless of differences in gender, ethnicity, or job role. Ultimately, each of us assesses the same factors—reliability, truth, and ability—when making our decision to trust, just like our ancestors have for tens of thousands of years. It's human nature.

And that's where this book comes in.

Our research has identified the crucial trust-building attitudes and behaviors that set the world's best managers apart from all others. These form the sixteen rules that, when followed, will have the greatest positive impact on your relationship with your employees, ensuring that they experience you as a reliable, truthful, and capable manager. The great news is that the rules are simple and surprisingly easy to live by. In fact, you may already do much of what I suggest in this book, and do it well. That's what makes you a *good* manager. But why settle for good when *great* is within your reach?

I'm not asking you to be someone you're not or to adopt dozens of new practices. Quite the opposite. Instead, I'm challenging you to think differently about how you manage your team. Continue to do most of the things that you already do, fine-tuning them based on the rules. If you feel that a suggestion is good but wouldn't suit your style or your team's culture, adapt it so that it feels right for you and them.

Some believe that having a successful career means finding the perfect manager and holding on. While that would be great, it's not how it works. The key to success in your career lies not in *finding* the perfect manager, but in *being* the perfect manager. In other words, focus less on any perceived shortcomings in your manager, and more on trying every day to *be* the type of manager that you yourself would wish to work for.

Trust Rules will help you to become the best manager that you can be by sharing evidence-based insights and practical tools used by some of the world's best managers to build the teams that together form the world's best workplaces. Take the time to incorporate these trust-building behaviors into your day-to-day management routine and I promise you that the results will be extraordinary and career defining. Tens of thousands of great managers around the world already know that *Trust Rules*.

Are you ready to join them? Great. Let's get to work.

RULE 1

TRUST FIRST

IMAGINE WHAT YOUR TEAM COULD achieve if your employees were to bring all of themselves—their skills, their talents, their imagination, their energy, their life experience, and their overall brilliance—to work every day. Think of the limitless potential that you would unleash if every member of your team was free to do their best work and share their best ideas, knowing that you value and respect them as unique individuals determined to leave their stamp on the world. That's the prize that's on offer when you trust your team. But only when you *fully* trust your team.

And that's the problem.

Trusting others is dangerous and risky because it leaves you exposed. Your trust can be taken for granted, abused, misused, unappreciated, and exploited. It can leave you looking foolish and naive. It can lead to poor-quality work, missed deadlines, and lost customers—for which you are ultimately responsible—reflecting badly on you as a manager and leaving you exposed to criticism from your peers and higher-ups. Or worse.

It's not difficult to understand, then, why so many managers traditionally have tried to achieve results by not trusting their employees, telling them everything that they should do rather than allowing them to decide some things for themselves. It's a familiar but thankfully fading soundtrack: the inspirational "your job is to do what I say"; the confidence-building "you better not mess this up"; and the reassuringly supportive "if you don't hear from me that means you're doing fine."

This command-and-control approach leaves nothing to chance, no disappointment, no failures, and no surprises. But there's a major downside to that approach. It leaves nothing to chance, no disappointment, no failures, and no surprises! In other words, you get exactly what you ask for: predictably average results but zero discretionary effort. Exactly what any other average manager can achieve.

There's another reason so many managers are hesitant to fully trust their employees: trusting others makes us vulnerable. And vulnerability can be extremely uncomfortable, particularly for those in a leadership role. We know that our teams need us to be strong, and we often assume that to be strong we must never show weakness or vulnerability.

As a manager, it would be wonderful if you could wait until each member of your team has shown themselves to be reliable, truthful, and able—and then trust them. But it doesn't work that way. For trust to take root, somebody must make the first move, so it's either them or you. Employees have little reason to take a chance on your trustworthiness and they are not all equally inclined to trust in general. Some of them are willing to trust quickly while others take longer to come around. Although an employee's opinion of you is obviously important in their decision to trust you, some of that decision has nothing to do with you and everything to do with the employee concerned.

Robert Hurley, a professor of management at New York's Fordham University, has identified ten factors that can predict if an individual will choose to trust or distrust another.[7] Five of Hurley's factors are worth a closer look here.

To start, an employee's *attitude toward risk* has a big impact on their willingness to trust you, or anyone. Risk seekers trust quickly. They don't spend much time figuring out what might go wrong if they trust you, because they believe that things will probably work out. But employees who are risk averse will be reluctant to place their trust in you unless they feel in control. "Not only do they not trust others," notes Hurley, "they don't even trust themselves."

An employee's *level of adjustment* also affects how long it takes them to build trust. Well-adjusted people tend to trust quickly—they are comfortable with themselves and with the world around them, and tend to believe that nothing bad will happen to them. A poorly adjusted employee, on the other hand, tends to see many threats in the world, approaches every situation with an underlying level of anxiety, and will take longer to trust you regardless of any good that you do.

Relative power is the third internal factor in an employee's decision to trust. You have the power in the relationship with each of your employees. That's just how it is. It's relatively easy for you to place your trust in employees because you hold all the cards. You can sanction them if they violate your trust. But what options do employees have if you betray them? They have no authority to do anything but withdraw their trust and resolve to be wiser in the future. Your employees instinctively understand this vulnerability and so will be less comfortable trusting you.

Another factor relevant to an employee's decision to trust is *security*. In other words, the key question for the employee is, *What's at stake?* "The higher the stakes, the less likely people are to trust," explains Hurley. "If the answer to the question, 'What's the worst that can happen?' isn't that scary, it's easier to be trustful." So, for example, employees are more likely to trust you when you are deciding on promotions than they are if you are considering layoffs.

Finally, according to Hurley, how *similar* you and your employees are also makes a big difference in their decision to trust you. We are all quicker to trust people that we can relate to, and we relate more easily to people "like us," people who share our values, interests, and perspective. People that are like you, then, are more likely to trust you. But while you might find it easier to earn the trust of a team built in your image, keep in mind that there's an important upside to diversity. McKinsey, the worldwide management consulting firm, reports that organizations with a diverse and inclusive workforce enjoy return on equity 53 percent higher and profit margins 14 percent greater than those of the least diverse companies.[8]

These five factors show just how challenging it is for employees to trust you and why they are unlikely to make the first move when it comes to building trust between you. They are more likely to wait and make their decision to trust based on how you perform over months or even years. But you don't have that luxury. You need trust if you are to unleash the full potential of your team. So, make the first move. Doing so doesn't make you weak. Your true strength lies in having the courage to show humility, openness, and a willingness to *trust first*.

Yes, being the first to extend trust is risky; it *can* go horribly wrong. But not if you go about it correctly. Problems typically arise when you extend *blind* trust, or when you trust and hope for the best, maybe better described as *foolish* trust. That's the sort of trust that will get you into trouble every time.

Imagine that your eighteen-year-old son asks for your help learning to drive. You trust him, and with good reason. He's a responsible teenager: he's worked a part-time job for years, takes good care of his siblings, and has always worked hard in school. You toss him the keys, saying, "Take my car, son. I trust you to figure out how it all works. You've never let me down before. Enjoy!" That's *blind, foolish* trust. Although your son has proven to be *trustworthy* in various situations, he has neither the training nor the competence to suggest that he can be trusted with your car. Your trust is unfair to him, as it's setting him up to fail. And it's unfair to you for the same reason.

Trust Rules is about extending *intelligent* trust: the right amount of trust given to the right person at the right time. For example, assigning a big project to an enthusiastic and capable but relatively new employee. Sharing confidential information about the company's performance with your employees. Allowing an employee to sign off on their colleagues' expenses when you're out of the office. Extending intelligent trust is a gradual process in which success breeds success and the inevitable setbacks are minor and controlled. You celebrate success, deal with setbacks, and carry on unfazed.

I opened this chapter by inviting you to imagine what your team could achieve if it could work at its full potential. It may sound fanciful, but it is both realistic and achievable when you fully trust yourself to fully trust your team. The rules in the rest of this book offer specific guidance on how to build trust with your employees. Rule 1, however, is the most important: trust first. You're the manager, so that's on you.

KEY POINTS

○ Being the first to trust leaves you exposed
  and makes you vulnerable—and it also
  shows your strength.

○ People tend to trust people who are like
  them. It's tempting to hire employees who
  are similar to you because they will likely be
  quicker to trust you. But be careful; you don't
  want to sacrifice the many benefits that a
  diverse team brings.

○ Don't trust your employees blindly. Instead,
  extend intelligent trust—the right amount
  of trust given to the right person at the right
  time.

RULE 2

LIVE WITH INTEGRITY

L IVING WITH INTEGRITY MEANS BEING true to your word in everything you do. It means that people can trust you because you do what you say. It's doing the right thing, even when no one is watching, and even if nobody would ever find out if you were to do the wrong thing. It means that you stand for something, even if you stand to lose everything in the process. In short, living with integrity reveals your true character. As the legendary basketball coach John Wooden said, "Be more concerned with your character than your reputation, because your character is what you really are, while your reputation is merely what others think you are."

In the workplace, integrity matters because how you conduct yourself with your employees, customers, vendors, and suppliers shows the standard of behavior you expect from them.

Most people have a strong sense of right and wrong and instinctively know the right thing to do when it's a simple black-or-white issue, but sometimes struggle when they encounter gray areas and borderline cases. Faced with uncertainty and moral dilemmas, your team will follow your lead. Act with the utmost integrity and you'll inspire your employees to do likewise. But when you compromise your integrity for commercial or personal advantage, you create space for others to do the same. The "right thing to do" is often also the "hard thing to do" and that's why, without strong leadership, some employees may yield to the temptation to take the path of least resistance.

Of course, you shouldn't do the right thing just to set a good example, or because your employees are watching you. You should do the right thing to show who you are, what you believe in, and the values that matter to you. When you live your values, what you do and what you say are one and the same. Even if you assume that most of your employees would do the right thing regardless of how you conduct yourself, they simply won't trust you if they don't see you holding yourself to the highest possible ethical standards. They will judge your behavior and attitudes, and each will form their own view on whether you are worthy of their trust.

Trust is about your reliability, which is based on your predictability—the degree to which your team can predict what you'll do or how you'll react in any situation. When employees know you as a person of integrity, one who tries to always do the right thing, you become easier to predict and therefore easier to trust. In short, the more strictly you adhere to a clear set of values, the more predictable—and reliable—you become in the eyes of your employees, and the more they will trust you.

Acting with integrity at work isn't always easy, though. There can be differences between actions that an organization considers to be OK and what you personally find acceptable. Just as we each develop values and morals that stay consistent over time, every organization has its own standards and codes of behavior, its own culture, "the way we do things around here."

You too have a "personal culture," what you stand for and what you believe in. Regardless of the culture of any organization for which you work, stay true to your personal culture. It's the violations of your personal code that will trouble your conscience, keep you awake at night, and ultimately damage your hard-earned reputation. In other words, while each organization has its own purpose and its own understanding of how to achieve that purpose, so do you. Don't ever be tempted to compromise your own values for the values of any employer.

Here are some practical ways you can act with integrity at work:

- *Be what you want your employees to be.* In other words, be fair in your daily decisions. Don't make excuses, point fingers, or blame others. Take responsibility for your mistakes and failures.

- *Be honest and ethical in everything you do.* Speak truthfully, be consistent and clear about your ethical standards, speak up even when it may be risky to do so, and challenge any system that encourages dishonesty or rewards unethical behavior.

- *Ensure that your team also works to the highest standards of ethical behavior.* Encourage people to speak up and express concerns about questionable practices. Review ethical concerns with your team.

- *Keep a positive and respectful attitude when challenging the status quo.* If you're right, let the power of your words win others over. Encourage and support others to voice their opinions, especially when their views challenge yours. Keep an open mind when you face objections—even when you sincerely believe that you're right, you just might be wrong.

- *Establish a code of values and behaviors that is unique to your team and to which every member can commit.* Set standards for the work duties of everyone on your staff and hold them accountable. If you hold them to a high standard, soon they'll hold themselves to a higher standard as well.

Living with integrity takes courage. Courage to speak up when your point of view is at odds with a senior leader's perspective or to challenge the status quo. Courage to turn down money-making opportunities that are ethically suspect. Courage to be different. And courage to risk personal loss when your personal code demands that you take a stand.

But living with integrity is worth the sacrifice. It takes years to build a good reputation, yet one ill-considered or poor decision can destroy it in seconds. You only have one reputation. Make it great. And make it last.

KEY POINTS

○ Your values are nonnegotiable. If a decision or an action doesn't feel right, it probably isn't. Don't compromise and don't try to silence your inner voice. Listen to it.

○ If it's a choice between organizational values and your own, back yourself. Real success begins with knowing who you truly are.

○ When it comes to matters of integrity, act as if the whole world is watching. Because it is.

RULE 3

KEEP YOUR PROMISES

HAVE YOU EVER BEEN IN a relationship with someone who doesn't keep their promises? If so, I doubt you would describe the relationship as good, and I'm positive that you wouldn't claim it was great. Why? Because none of us can trust a person who is inconsistent or acts unpredictably. And if you can't rely on a person, nothing worthwhile is possible. The fact that they sometimes deliver counts for nothing because it's always preceded by uncertainty and often followed by disappointment. Like a dog who only bites you sometimes.

So why are so many managers not as dependable as they'd like to be? Why do so many of them fail to do what they say they will do? Because promises are like babies: easy to make, but hard to deliver.

Most managers keep their big promises. Employees expect to be paid in full and on time every month—and they usually are. If they're promised an annual performance appraisal, it usually happens. And when an application for vacation is approved, they generally get to take that time off.

The problem lies mainly with the *small* promises. Or *broken* small promises, to be precise. The barely noticed, casual, I-can't-believe-you'd-even-consider-that-a-promise promises. Few managers purposely set out to mislead their employees; the issue is that managers and employees often have different interpretations of what constitutes a promise. Like beauty, the promise is in the eye of the beholder. Like it or not, it's a promise if your *employee* takes it as a promise. Most of us make promises without even realizing that we're doing so. And because we don't see them as promises, we may not keep them.

"Let's meet at ten" is a promise.

"I'll ask Mike to train you on that process" is a promise.

"I'll let you know in five minutes" is a promise.

"Let me think about it" is a promise.

"I'll talk to my boss and let you know" is a promise.

"I'll arrange for you to be invited to our weekly pro-duction meeting" is a promise.

It's no coincidence that many of these promises involve meeting a deadline or making time for employ-ees and their requests. Managers are busy, usually work-ing under time pressure, and time is what we need most but have the least. But that's a fact of life, not an excuse.

So, what can you do to make sure that you keep all your promises—big and small? Napoleon Bonaparte had a point when he said, "The best way to keep one's word is not to give it." It sounds cynical, but if you make fewer promises you'll also *break* fewer promises. Remember that what may be just an offhand comment by you might be heard by your employee as a serious promise and taken at face value. So, pause and think about these things before you make a promise:

- *Ask yourself, "What's really needed here?"* before *you make your promise.* We often overpromise out of a genuine desire to help, to go the extra mile. So, we commit to giving an answer "by the end of the day" when "by the end of the week" might have been equally acceptable. Underpromise and overdeliver. It's a cliché—but no less true because of it.

- *Clarify your promise.* Leave no room for doubt or ambiguity about exactly what you are committing to. Take time to confirm mutual understanding of what you are promising. Otherwise, you can succeed in delivering what *you* understood you'd promised, yet leave the other person feeling let down and disappointed that you didn't deliver what *they* heard you promise.

- *Write every promise down.* We break some promises because they were unrealistic to begin with. We break others because we didn't even realize that we were making a commitment. And we break some promises because of a change in circumstances, such as an illness, an emergency, or another unforeseen situation. But often, we break them simply because we forget. Jot down the commitments you make on your planner or your calendar, or keep a separate list—whatever works best for you. In any case, write them down in the same place all the time and review your list regularly to make sure that nothing slips through.

Your ability to keep your promises sometimes depends on other people keeping promises they've made to you. If you're not confident that they'll deliver on their promises to you in full and on time, make allowances for that in any commitments that you make to your team. You can only control delivery of *your* promises. You can try to influence your colleagues to deliver on theirs, but their failures must not become your excuses, because your team will hold you responsible for the commitments you break—even when it's not your fault.

In all circumstances, if you genuinely can't deliver on a promise you've made, let your employee know as soon as possible. Most of us don't mind an occasional broken promise; it's the silence or the feigned ignorance or the indifference that upsets us. If you honestly have no choice but to break a commitment, let the other person know at the first opportunity. If you are normally reliable, they will probably give you the benefit of the doubt and treat it as a commitment postponed rather than a promise broken. If you've had to break a promise, think twice before giving a fresh commitment to make up for it—and break *that* promise at your peril. We all realize eventually that a promise is only as dependable as the person who makes it, and none of us can trust a person that we can't depend on. That's just how it is.

KEY POINTS

○ Think before you promise. To break fewer
   promises, make fewer promises. Better
   a simple "no" today than a long apology
   tomorrow.

○ Clarify the promise. Make sure that you
   each have a shared understanding of your
   commitment.

○ If you have no alternative but to break a
   promise, let anyone affected know as soon as
   you possibly can.

RULE 4

BE APPROACHABLE AND EASY TO TALK TO

THE QUALITY OF ALMOST EVERY workplace relationship is decided by how well the people involved can communicate with each other.

Communication is the act of passing information, ideas, or thoughts from one person to another. It's also the process by which we reach *understandings* with each other. When we say that we enjoy "good communication" with each other, we mean—at face value—that we are good at exchanging information, ideas, and thoughts. But what we really mean is not so much that we understand the *words* that the other person uses, but that we "get" each other. So, when we talk about the quality of two-way communication in the workplace, we mean the extent to which people understand and get each other.

Effective two-way communication lies at the heart of the high-trust workplace. Almost every aspect of every relationship thrives when communication is good, while poor two-way communication makes everything more difficult and some things impossible. Many problems that appear at first to be symptomatic of something else have their roots in poor communication. For example, when employees complain about the unfairness of promotions, or disappointing pay raises, or unreasonable allocations of work, or anything else "unfair," it is almost inevitable that the root cause of the problem—and, therefore, the *real* problem—is poor communication.

The key to effective two-way communication between you and each of your employees is to be approachable. You already create opportunities to talk to your team, like one-on-one check-ins or team meetings. Those opportunities are important and valuable, but you control them and what gets talked about. Because conversations started by your employees have a different dynamic, those employees must be comfortable approaching you, confident that if they need to talk to you about something important, you'll give them the time and attention they need.

When your employees regard you as being approachable and easy to talk to, they are much more likely to start a discussion with you. The relaxed conversations that follow help you develop a closeness that goes beyond the designated "manager-employee" arrangement—a key distinguishing feature of a high-trust workplace relationship.

Your approachability doesn't only help your employees. Because you can't be everywhere at once, you need your team members to be your eyes and ears, and they need to know that they can share concerns and alert you to minor issues before they become major ones. If you're hard to approach, there's a bigger risk that employees will leave you in the dark if things go wrong, involving you only when a problem has already escalated.

Like most managers, you probably claim to have an open-door policy to let employees know they can approach you anytime. (This is a safe bet: I've yet to hear a manager boast of a "closed-door" policy.) Yet despite the prevalence of open-door policies and the availability that they signal, employees consistently complain that it's hard to talk to their managers.

What's going on?

Access is less about your door being open, and more about your *mind* being open. You are probably much less available to your team than you think because, regardless of whether you tell your employees they have access to you or keep your door open, you show your unavailability with your body language and actions. When you always *appear* busy rushing from one meeting to the next, or when you grimace subtly when an employee asks for a minute of your time, your body language sends a clear message: I don't have time for you. When you scan your e-mails while watching an employee give a presentation or while "listening" to an employee's question, your multitasking suggests that you're not really interested in what the employee has to say.

Your full attention is essential for a successful conversation. How do you feel when a colleague keeps glancing back to their screen or over your shoulder while you're asking for their advice about a challenging issue? Do you feel that they care, that they're interested and want to help? Hardly! When you give your employee anything other than your full, undivided attention, your message is, "I've got important things to think about right now—and you're not one of them."

If an employee approaches you and "now" is not a good time, suggest a better time to talk. Otherwise, stop what you're doing, sit back, relax, and enjoy the conversation. The message you should send is, "There is nothing else that I'd rather do right now than talk with you." Giving employees your full attention when they ask to talk to you creates a win-win-win. You get to hear what's on your employee's mind, they get to feel heard, and you both get to feel good.

Being approachable isn't about sitting on your throne waiting to receive your employees—it's about employees feeling comfortable enough to approach you and start a conversation anywhere. To be truly accessible, don't wait for your employees to seek you out—instead, go to them.

One popular approach is the rather unscientific-sounding "management by wandering around," or MBWA—a business management style in which managers wander around the workplace in a random and unstructured manner to keep up-to-date on what's happening in the business and to check in on the people who are making success happen. Whether your team members are in one place or multiple locations, get out there so you can better understand and act on their issues, ideas, and concerns. Be visible. Here's how:

- *Consistently reserve time to get away from your desk and walk through your department.* Do you even need an office? Could you have a desk on the floor with everyone else? Or, if you're responsible for people in multiple locations, can you base yourself in each location at various times?

- *Make yourself available for impromptu discussions.* As you walk around, be willing to listen, answer questions honestly, and ask intelligent questions of your own that are designed to help you understand your team better.

- *Create opportunities for chatting over a meal.* Hold regular face-to-face lunch or breakfast meetings with small groups of employees. Some managers host "open mic" lunches at which they make it clear that no questions are off-limits. Until employees are confident enough to fully embrace this concept, bring a few questions of your own, such as, "What keeps me awake at night?" or "What are the biggest threats we are currently facing?" to set a tone of candor and openness.

The open-door policy and MBWA have one thing in common: an approachable manager who is easy to talk to. Being easy to talk to or approachable, however, involves feeling comfortable chatting with your employees and colleagues. For some managers this is easy, while others may find it one of the harder things that they must do each day. For example, talking to others usually comes naturally to extroverts, while introverts must push themselves hard to close the gap between goodwill and good communication.

Of course, most of us are neither fully an extrovert or an introvert, but somewhere in between. Regardless of where you fall on the scale, use your strengths and manage your weaknesses so that you become the best two-way communicator that you can be while still being relatively comfortable in your own skin and fully authentic. If you feel uncomfortable or have difficulty talking with your employees, follow these few simple techniques to help you improve your conversations:

- *Smile.* Nothing says that you are open and approachable as much as a sincere smile. A smile is worth a thousand words.

- *Share.* Sharing information or stories often helps others see you as approachable and helps to build trust and relationships. Small tidbits of your life outside work will do perfectly; you don't have to confess your family secrets.

- *Watch your nonverbal communication.* Reserved managers sometimes appear disinterested or distracted because they show few signs of listening. Practice your communication cues and clues. It's not enough to listen; you must be seen listening. Nod your head in agreement. Maintain eye contact. Ask questions and check for understanding.

- *Manage your "talk-to-listen" ratio.* This ratio is the time you spend talking in any given conversation versus the time you spend listening. For example, when outlining your vision of the future for the team, your ratio will be high; you'll do most, if not all, of the talking. But if an employee needs your advice on something that's worrying them, your ratio should be much lower because you should be doing lots of listening. If you're known as a talker and typically take up about 80 percent of the airtime, you'll get much better results if you talk just 60 percent of the time and listen for 40 percent instead of just 20. Talk less, listen more.

- *Talk when* they *are listening.* Jeff Shore, a sales expert and author, suggests assuming you have the other person's attention "for no more than thirty seconds without any input from them." According to Shore, "This is when your 'light' is completely green. From thirty to sixty seconds, you are in the 'yellow light' zone; maybe they are listening, maybe they aren't. Talk sixty seconds or longer without interaction, and you're in the 'red light' zone; you've lost them."[9]

We live in a busy world and there are never quite enough hours in the day to do everything we set out to do. As tempting as it may seem to "be efficient" by keeping our heads down and our doors closed, by multitasking when talking to others or rushing through a conversation, we are actually less productive. If you truly want to be effective and save time, be accessible to your most valuable assets—your employees—and make it easy for them to talk to you. Above all: be a good listener.

KEY POINTS

○ Be fully present when talking and listening to your employees.

○ Get away from your desk and talk informally with your people every day.

○ Be authentic in your communication style. Your personality is a feature, not an excuse, and there's no personality type that can't succeed at communicating effectively with others.

RULE 5

GIVE STRAIGHT ANSWERS

ANSWER YOUR EMPLOYEES' QUESTIONS CLEARLY and fully. This saves them having to decipher your answers and figure out what you are really saying, leaving them free to focus their efforts on their work.

Even when you must give employees information they won't like, it's better to be straightforward than to be indirect or play for time. Your team—often without being consciously aware of it—are constantly evaluating if what you say matches what you do. By giving truthful answers, you show that you place a high value on being honest and straightforward and you inspire them to do likewise.

Straight talk takes courage, and maybe that explains why some of us are evasive or economical with the truth from time to time. Why do we sometimes find it hard to be direct and straightforward? Often, we don't want to disappoint our employees with bad news. While this reluctance is understandable, it is usually wrong. When you explain the reasons behind a decision they may not like, your employees will at least understand it, and walk away with the sense that you are treating everyone fairly.

Some managers feel uncomfortable giving anything other than positive feedback and so they sometimes lie, emphasizing the positive and downplaying the negative, hoping to spare their employees' feelings. While tact is certainly necessary when offering constructive feedback, it's critical that employees learn the truth—or enough of the truth—to improve in the future.

Sometimes managers play for time. Faced with a troubling or uncertain situation that could adversely affect their team, they say little or nothing about it, hoping that circumstances will improve. Such equivocation or outright silence damages trust and extracts a heavy price in the long run. To maintain trust, deliver positive and negative news with equal speed and equal honesty.

Knowledge is power. For example, when you know how to do something that others don't, or when you know something that your employee doesn't, you have power. That's why in lower-trust workplaces, managers often closely guard whatever information they have, believing that it protects their position and gives them an edge. It seldom does either. Hoarding information rarely pays off because the best way to leverage information is almost always to share it generously.

Share information about a problem with your team and you might get suggestions or possible solutions to it. Tell employees about the wider organization's weak performance or a discouraging business environment, and your employees will understand what's going on outside your department and won't be blindsided by the news. Sometimes managers even withhold *good* financial news for fear that employees will use it to extract advantage. For example, if the company has done exceptionally well in the previous year, you might fear that employees will seek pay raises or bonuses. But if pay levels are already fair and you offer a reasonable explanation of how and why the organization plans to use the extra revenue, high-trust employees will understand.

Managers sometimes withhold information from their employees out of concern about what would happen if it were to "get out" in the media. This may be a legitimate concern if the information is only commercially sensitive. But if it's information that would show the organization in a bad light if exposed, rather than ask, "How can I keep this out of the media?" shouldn't the manager be asking, "Why are we doing something that we don't want the public to know about?"

A high-trust manager always gives straight answers. But note that being straightforward with your employees is not the same as always giving them the information that they request. There are many circumstances where you might choose not to or are restricted from doing so: when the answer would require exposing sensitive financial information; personal or work-related information about you or another employee; or information that is, frankly, just none of that person's business.

Inevitably, there will be times when you are not free to share information that you have, and, obviously, at those times you must respect the trust that others have placed in you and keep that information confidential, no matter how difficult it is or how uncomfortable you feel. But don't let secrecy be your default position. Be open, keeping information secret only when it's specified, requested, or clearly the most sensible thing to do.

If you don't know the answer to a question or can't divulge certain information, say so and expand a little so as not to leave employees totally in the dark. For example, say, "I don't have that information, but I will find it and share it with you," or "I have that information, but I can't share it with you right now because . . ." You're a manager, not a politician, so share what you know and are permitted to share—not what you think you can get away with.

It's good to give an answer when asked, but even better to volunteer that information without waiting to be asked. Communicate proactively. High-trust managers are generous when it comes to when and what they share. Keep your team informed about important issues and changes. Update them often so they receive information about issues that affect their jobs and the business.

Make sure, however, that you don't overload your people with too much information. Aim to strike a balance between too little and too much. Share too little, and you create the suspicion that something is going on. Share too much, and you can cause confusion. But more importantly, you can cause people to disengage. If it's too much trouble to work through the information that comes their way, many people just won't bother, meaning that the important stuff gets buried among the less important details. So how do you find the right level? Listen to your team—they'll tell you how you're doing.

Sometimes what you leave out is more important than what you share. For example, a group of employees at a large company heard rumors that one of their branches would soon close. But their manager reassured them that there was no truth whatsoever to the rumors. A few weeks later, the employees were stunned to learn that the branch—while remaining open—would cease to offer a full range of services, and that two-thirds of the employees at that location would lose their jobs.

When confronted, the manager justified his earlier statement on the basis that he had told his employees, truthfully, that the branch would not close! While it is true that the employees did not ask "the right question"— whether the company planned to scale back operations at that branch and how many jobs would be lost—a high-trust manager would never try to excuse withholding information because of the way a question was phrased. Whether it's a straightforward lie or a lie of omission (leaving out an important piece of information), it's still a lie. If you know more than you are at liberty to share, tell them that. Straight talk is as much about the information you volunteer *without* being asked as what you offer when asked.

KEY POINTS

○ Don't wait to be asked. Communicate proactively.

○ It's not only what you say that matters—what you *don't* say is also important. Creating a misleading impression by purposely omitting important information is simply lying by a different name, and both impact trust in the same way.

○ Be clear and generous in the information you share. You can't have trust without truth.

RULE 6

Seek and Respond to Suggestions and Ideas

According to professors Alan Robinson and Dean Schroeder's *The Idea-Driven Organization,* about 80 percent of an organization's potential for improvement lies in soliciting innovative ideas from frontline workers.[10] That's not surprising. Employees see what's working well and what can be improved. They experience firsthand the frustrations that their customers feel. They witness the lost opportunities and the waste of effort, resources, and money. As true experts in their jobs, they often have great suggestions for how to improve efficiency, save money, enhance customer service, and boost productivity. Many employees wish that someone would show interest in their ideas. But others stopped caring a long time ago.

Many companies have employee-suggestion programs that encourage employees to offer their advice, but, sadly, a great many of these programs just don't work for anyone.

So, why do suggestion schemes fail?

Some ask employees for too much information in support of their suggestion or idea. Employees might be told to outline their idea in exhaustive detail, or give supporting technical or financial information to which they have no access. Other programs don't allow employees to report a problem or offer feedback on an issue unless they also have a solution, meaning that many problems go unreported despite the possibility that another employee or team might have the answer. Finally, some programs flounder because they don't excite or engage with employees.

Managers are also often reluctant to seek their employees' input or opinions because they don't know how to process and make sense of the information they might receive—and they worry that they will upset the employee that offered the input if they challenge the employee's ideas.

In general, the demise of suggestion programs tends to follow a predictable pattern, and at its root is a failure by management to acknowledge, consider, or act upon employees' ideas.

At first, honored to be asked, employees enthusiastically submit their ideas. Although the organization might implement a few suggestions, most are ignored, causing many employees to resolve to keep their next great idea to themselves. Or worse, they disengage. They cease to care much about the recurring problems or lost opportunities that they might previously have highlighted, telling themselves "it's not my problem" or "if management wants to know, they'll ask."

It's not difficult to understand why a manager might choose to ignore a suggestion or idea and hope that it'll go away. Some suggestions are impractical or unworkable, while others can charitably be described as "poorly thought through." I understand why a busy manager might be tempted to bury the sheaf of suggestions at the back of a filing cabinet, rather than take time to tease them out further with the employee or give direct and honest feedback on why the suggestion can't be implemented. But that's not the solution.

Here's how you can avoid this scenario:

Before you first approach employees for their input, think about what you want to know from them. The quality of the question you ask will dictate the quality of the answer you get. Use open questions to generate thoughtful answers. Focus the employees' sights on a large challenge (for example, how to cut international shipping costs) or ask for insights to a specific problem (say, recurring stock shortages).

Ask for only the minimum amount of information needed to convey their ideas or suggestions. If you find an idea intriguing, you can always go back and ask for more detail. Welcome information about problems the employees see in the workplace, even when no solution is apparent. Just knowing that a problem exists is half the battle.

Engage your people—individually or in small groups—and invite them to share their suggestions on how things could be done better. Offer multiple ways to contribute so that each employee can use the channel that suits them best. Some will be excited to tease their ideas out face-to-face with you while others will prefer the perceived distance that e-mail offers. If employees already make suggestions at staff meetings and in day-to-day conversations, stick with what works rather than launching or trying to resuscitate a more formal employee-suggestion program.

If other managers have tried and failed with similar employee-suggestion initiatives in the past, don't ignore that fact. Explain to your employees that you want to tap into their expert knowledge, acknowledge the failings of the past, and ask them to tell you how they would like to contribute their ideas and insights in the future.

Asking is easy. It's the follow-up that's hard. Don't ask for your employees' input if you don't want to know what they think. Don't ask unless you're fully committed to responding to their suggestions and to letting them know how you plan to use their input. Otherwise, you'll just demoralize the team, leaving them wishing they had kept their ideas to themselves. Promise that when you can't implement a suggestion, you will always let them know the reason why. Even if an idea is impractical or unworkable, your team will respect your straight talk and honest feedback. Your active pursuit of their suggestions and ideas will enhance the sense of trust and collaboration in your workplace.

KEY POINTS

○ If you want great answers, start by asking great questions. Open-ended questions generate thoughtful answers. Closed ones don't.

○ Don't wait for inspiration to strike. Encourage employees to generate solutions and ideas through brainstorming, and give them the opportunity to develop their best ideas further.

○ Give feedback on every suggestion offered no matter how outlandish it might be. Be constructive, truthful, and sensitive.

RULE 7

Involve People in Decisions That Affect Them

CHANGE IS INEVITABLE IN EVERY company and business—and can be hard for those affected by it. Often, it's not the change itself that upsets people, but the perceived lack of control or influence over events that result from the change.

High-trust managers understand this, and create opportunities for employees to take part in the decision-making process on matters that affect their jobs or workplace. Employees who are involved in this way develop a better understanding of why decisions are made and an appreciation of the responsibility that goes hand in hand with making these decisions. They develop a deeper sense of ownership of their work and a sense of responsibility for the successful implementation of changes because they've been closely involved in shaping them.

It should almost always be possible to allow employees at least some say in decisions that will affect them. Sadly, it seems to rarely happen, which is puzzling. Employees have the greatest knowledge of what's involved in doing their jobs, and therefore also tend to have good ideas about how to fix or improve processes or issues related to them. Seeking employees' input on major decisions that will affect them makes solid business sense, but it is also the right and respectful thing to do.

For example, great workplaces aren't immune to economic downturns and many have had to resort to wage cuts or layoffs at some point in their pasts. These economic downturns are times of unusual uncertainty: circumstances can change daily or hourly, managers often have little information but are expected to have all the answers, and a general sense of doom can settle over a workplace. I have been privileged to work closely with many great organizations as they worked through such challenging times, and it's been fascinating to see how they have acted in times of great pressure. For example, when faced with the decision to cut wages or lay off people, rather than hide or plead ignorance, high-trust managers in those great workplaces involved their employees from the outset. They shared what they knew with them, and were honest about what they didn't know. They explained the pressures and challenges of the situation candidly, and looked for input and possible solutions from their people.

And employees didn't let them down. Some suggested across-the-board reductions in hours to prevent any layoffs. Other teams suggested wage cuts to reduce costs. Many organizations managed to cut costs without cutting employee numbers or payroll through myriad employee-driven initiatives. As these examples show, employees' willingness to work with their managers to find acceptable solutions is a direct result of the respect shown to those employees in the past. Think of it as a trust reservoir that both management and employees can top up and dip into at various times. The deeper the reservoir, the greater your capacity to draw on the accumulated trust in times of need.

So, next time a major change or decision looms, look for input from your team. Involve them in any decision that affects the job that they do: how their work is done, organized, scheduled, and assigned, or the environment in which they work.

Proactively share as much information as you possibly can, being sure to tell them if you have other information that you can't share right now. Explain the circumstances that have led to this decision-making point or that made changes necessary. Look for their input—but only on those aspects that they can genuinely influence. If you have already decided on an issue, don't pretend that the outcome is still up for discussion. Instead, explain the final decision and why you made it, and outline what is still open for discussion. For example, extended opening hours might be nonnegotiable, but perhaps the team can take responsibility for shaping the revised employee schedules. Or, when budgets change, the new sales target might be fixed, but you can explore options for reaching it with the team.

Every employee should have the opportunity to be involved in discussions and group decisions, but not all employees have the necessary skills and experience to contribute fully. Less experienced participants may not fully grasp the issues at hand or know enough yet to be able to figure out which of several options to choose. Don't expect the same level of contribution from, say, an employee fresh out of college as from a more experienced employee familiar with the organization and its business priorities.

Also, accept that not everyone *wants* to be involved in decision-making to the same extent. Some employees will embrace the opportunity enthusiastically, while others will be reluctant to contribute. While respecting each employee's right to be involved only to the extent that they wish, encourage the widest possible participation. Your crowd becomes less wise as it shrinks in size, because fewer opinions and perspectives are available to the group.

Remember that involving employees in decision-making is not the same as "collective decision-making." Employee involvement means that you look for input from your team and take that input fully into account when making your decision. But *you* make the decision. Collective decision-making is quite different, implying that the group will make the decision together. That's not what I'm suggesting. Managers manage. And that means having the ultimate say in—and taking complete responsibility for—decisions.

What's the downside to involving employees in decision-making? Involving employees takes more of your time up front. Groups need more time to consider issues, which can slow down your decision-making. Your ability to respond quickly enough to a change of circumstances may be compromised.

Also, getting more people involved in key decisions inevitably means sharing relevant data and information, some of which may be sensitive and confidential. Understandably, you may have concerns about employees talking about these things outside your group or the organization—the more people that know sensitive information, the greater the risk of it getting out. And there's the challenge of precedent—once you've started to involve employees in making some decisions, you risk damage to morale and commitment if you exclude them from making others.

But, overwhelmingly, the benefits of involving employees in decision-making significantly outweigh the risks and potential downsides. Often, employees resist change because they don't understand why that change is being implemented or how it will affect their professional and personal lives in the future. But if you give employees the opportunity to participate in a decision that will affect them, you will also help them to understand why the change that inevitably follows is necessary, and you will get them on board faster.

More importantly, when you involve employees in the decision-making process, your employees will know that you value them and they will do whatever it takes to ensure the success of the team. When employees have a complete picture of their team, the wider organization, and the decisions their managers must grapple with, they make smarter day-to-day decisions. Because employees feel a sense of ownership of key decisions and a deeper understanding of why they were made, they don't waste energy criticizing or disowning decisions that don't turn out as planned. Instead, they work hard to put things right. And morale and motivation is higher because employees know they make a difference to the team's success.

It takes time and energy to involve your employees in the decision-making process, but this collaborative approach offers so much more potential than the alternative: management by decree.

KEY POINTS

○ When it's necessary to make tough decisions, ask your employees for input—but only on those aspects of the decision that they can genuinely influence.

○ Involving employees in the decision-making process means that you ask for their input—not that they make the decision. Take their input fully into account, but, as the manager, you make the final decision.

○ Not all employees have the skills and experience to weigh in on decision-making—and not every employee wants to take part in the process. Respect people's limitations and willingness to participate, but encourage as many people as possible to contribute.

RULE 8

MAKE YOUR EXPECTATIONS CLEAR

DO YOUR EMPLOYEES KNOW WHAT you expect of them? Have you sat down with them and explained your expectations for each of their core responsibilities? Have you shared with them specific examples of what great performance in their role would look like? And if you've done these things, are you confident that their understanding of those expectations matches yours?

Your employees need to know what you expect of them. In fact, they have the *right* to know, because how else can they succeed in their role? When they understand your expectations, your employees can set their goals, choose the right priorities, and trust that they know where they stand with you.

Your expectations of each employee fall into two categories: formal and informal. The formal expectations of a role are typically expressed as SMART performance objectives: Specific, Measurable, Agreed-Upon, Realistic, and Time-Based (that is, they have a clear deadline or schedule). You also have informal, day-to-day expectations about how employees should behave, collaborate, and interact with each other. Ultimately, your employees need to know the answers to the following four questions:

- *What do you expect of me?* Before you tell employees your expectations of them, write those expectations down. If you can't write them down clearly, you can't share them clearly, and you certainly can't expect your employees to understand them. Start by developing meaningful job descriptions and performance objectives that accurately describe the expectations you have for your employees. Review them with your employees from time to time to keep the goals current and relevant to the work employees are actually doing. Set these objectives and expectations in the context of the bigger picture, so employees understand the impact that their performance will have on the team's success. Make sure they have the necessary skills, experience, ability, and attitude to succeed. Finally, in every conversation about these objectives, check that your employees truly understand what your expectations are.

- *How am I doing?* Give continuous feedback. Sit down regularly with each employee to talk about your expectations. Don't shy away from offering honest feedback when an employee's performance falls short of the expectations you set for them. Even star employees occasionally need help and feedback to stay on course.

- *Where do I stand?* While ongoing feedback will help employees in their day-to-day tasks, you also need to let them know in a structured manner how their overall performance stacks up against the expectations you set. I've yet to find the perfect performance-review system, but regardless of any shortcomings yours has, use it. Properly. Each employee has expectations—created when they were introduced to the program—around objectives, appraisal, development, and career progression, and it's your responsibility to ensure those expectations are met.

- *How can I improve?* It's not enough to tell your employees what they are doing wrong or highlight areas in which they are falling short of expectations. Tell them *how* to do better and help them close those gaps through coaching or training.

Don't rely exclusively on one-on-one sessions with individual employees to set expectations and measure performance. Hold regular, short meetings with your team as well, to review departmental goals, team efforts, and future projects. Communicate expectations to the full team at the same time. Ask for ideas and feedback, and take them on board. Your team will appreciate your flexibility when you adjust your expectations based on their honest feedback, and they will work hard to achieve objectives that they—and you—know to be both realistic and fair.

KEY POINTS

○ Sit down regularly with each employee to talk about your expectations and share your ideas about what great performance looks like in that role.

○ Check understanding by periodically asking employees to tell you what *they* think you expect from them, and what *they* think success in their role looks like.

○ If your company has a formal performance-appraisal system, use it.

RULE 9

SHOW A WARM WELCOME

YOU'VE FOUND THE PERFECT PERSON to join your team. Think of the effort you invested in finding them, to make sure that they're just the right fit. Now make double that effort to extend the warmest, friendliest, and most legendary welcome imaginable. This is their big day. Show them that it's a big day for you too!

For you and your colleagues, it may be business as usual except that a new person is joining your team. But for your new hire, today is the culmination of a process that has spanned months. Spotting the job opportunity. Thinking about it. Completing the application process, then the selection process, and then the grueling waiting process, before finally receiving the great news: they got the job. Congratulations!

Now the "first day" questions start. What's the dress code? How long should they allow to commute to your premises? Will their boss be nice? Will they get along with their coworkers? There are many more questions and decisions and plans to make. For the new hire, contemplating the first day at the job is likely a mix of uncertainty and nervousness, coupled with large doses of excitement, energy, and enthusiasm.

Then the first day arrives. Balloon burst. Excitement and enthusiasm turn to awkward embarrassment when your new employee realizes that no one seems to have been expecting them. Twenty minutes waiting in the lobby while the receptionist tries to reach someone to look after . . . "What did you say your name is?" An hour sitting at a desk waiting for you to finish your meetings, all the while smiling awkwardly at curious strangers. Wondering where the bathroom is, but afraid to explore in case you come looking for them. And everyone is wearing jeans—they feel like they're dressed for a wedding. Or a funeral. Theirs.

I've exaggerated a little to make my point. But sadly, this is an accurate description of the sort of welcome that awaits many new hires. There are other variations, of course. The "read this manual all day to get an idea of what we do" welcome. The "sit with John this week and watch what he does" welcome. The "join us for lunch, but when you arrive at the table, there is no place for you" welcome.

There *is* a better way to minimize a new hire's uncertainty, ease their nervousness, share their excitement, and feed their enthusiasm. You just need a plan. Let's explore a few ideas.

START WITH A WELCOME STRATEGY

Develop and document a strategy designed to ensure new hires feel comfortable, accepted, and welcome from the moment they learn that they got the job. Gather your team and encourage them to chat about *their* first-day memories to generate ideas on how best to welcome a new person into your team. Explore what went well and what could have been better. Assemble a small team to run the project, including long-serving employees for their experience and practicality and recent new hires for their empathy and enthusiasm. Everyone has a personal stake in making sure these promising new hires settle in as quickly as possible and stick around. After all, if they only last a few weeks in the job, their leaving will affect everyone on the team.

WELCOME YOUR NEW EMPLOYEE
BEFORE THEIR FIRST DAY

Call the new hire a week or so before they are due to
start. Be enthusiastic and welcoming. Run through the
basic information that they'll need—when and where to
show up, the dress code, and the plan for their first day.
Encourage them to ask any questions, no matter how
trivial they might consider them to be. Drop them an
e-mail immediately afterward to confirm the details and
give answers to any questions that came up in your call.

Also, consider meeting them for coffee or lunch
before they start, possibly with a few of their new colleagues, to soothe any nerves your new employee might
be experiencing. This visit gives them a chance to meet
the team in a social setting and talk about things other
than work, and it ensures that on their first day, they'll
already know some of their new colleagues.

Arrange your new hire's e-mail address as soon
as they accept your job offer. Then, encourage everyone on your team to write a short e-mail to introduce
themselves and welcome their new teammate on board.
Imagine your new employee's surprise when they log in
for the first time—it will probably be the only time in
their career when they'll be delighted and grateful to find
an overflowing inbox. Also, make sure they'll have all the

basics, such as a desk and chair, a working phone, and any necessary security cards or key swipes on their first day.

MAKE SURE THEY'RE WELCOMED ON THEIR FIRST DAY

Who will greet them when they arrive? Often, the first person a new employee will meet on their first day will be the receptionist or the security guard. Let those employees know that your new hire is expected. Show them a photo and tell them the new employee's name and role. Encourage them to welcome this new member to the organization so that when they ask for you at reception, they're greeted with warm recognition ("I'm guessing that you're Mary? Welcome to the team!"). Won't that make them feel welcome, special, and valued?

Be there. You're their boss. Welcoming your new employee personally is more important than anything else you could possibly do and anyone else you could possibly meet at that time. There's no rule that says you must ask a new hire to show up first thing on a Monday. If you have too much going on at the start of the week, just ask them to start on Tuesday. And if your first hour is always hectic, ask them to show up midmorning. Just be there, ready to give them your undivided attention.

Meet them at reception, and escort them in. Don't keep them waiting.

DEVELOP A SOCIAL AND WORK PLAN

Coffee breaks and lunchtimes can be a problem for many new hires. If they're lucky, they will have empathetic colleagues who will make a point of including them. If you are sure that this will happen in your workplace, great. But if you have any concerns, don't leave it to chance.

Plan your new team member's first week. Make a roster. It's as simple as sending an e-mail to your team asking when they'd like to have lunch or take a break with their new colleague. It might sound contrived—and maybe it is—but it's not half as tortuous as a first week dogged by the embarrassment of dining alone or trying to infiltrate established groups. After you've done this for a few new hires, it will take on a life of its own as those who you welcomed in this way will want to do the same for their new colleagues.

Take the employee around and personally introduce them to the rest of the company (or department, depending on the size of your operation). Or develop a buddy system. Carefully choose someone to show the new person around, explain how things work and who does what, ensure that they have opportunities to meet their colleagues over lunch and coffee breaks, and offer support and guidance as needed.

Get the new employee working productively as quickly as possible to help them transition mentally from outsider to team member. Invite them to meetings that relate to their area of responsibility and help them get involved. Be sure to ask for and listen carefully to their input—if meetings are usually fast-paced and energetic, give them your support and encouragement while they settle in and adjust to the prevailing culture. And of course, involve them in all the social activities around the workplace.

Remember that it's equally important to welcome people who have changed roles or who join your team from another part of the organization. Managers often overlook this part of the initial welcoming process, which makes it more valuable and appreciated when it happens.

AN INVESTMENT FOR LIFE

You will never have a greater opportunity to channel a new team member's energy, enthusiasm, and commitment—maybe even to capture it for life—than you will on their first day. By extending a warm welcome and helping them to settle in, you send a strong signal of the value that you place on this person, promoting positive levels of camaraderie and deeper levels of engagement from day one.

It's surprisingly easy to develop and implement a welcome strategy that will make an enormous difference in how a new employee experiences your organization—practices that will have them telling family and friends and anyone who will listen about their wonderful new job with an incredible organization and the most welcoming people they have ever met. Because most organizations get it so wrong, people talk about those that get it right.

KEY POINTS

○ Ease your new hire's anxiety about their first day by reaching out to them in advance. In this case, familiarity breeds *contentment*.

○ Don't leave your new hire's first days to chance; plan them carefully. You never get a second chance to make a first impression.

○ Remember that a new hire isn't always necessarily "new" to the organization. Make sure you extend an equally thoughtful and warm welcome to employees joining you from within the company. It's a great opportunity to set the tone for this next stage of their career and to show them what makes your team special.

RULE 10

Nobody's Job Is "Just" Anything

NOBODY ON YOUR TEAM IS unimportant or irrelevant. Nobody should feel less a part of the team than anybody else, whether they work full- or part-time, have twenty years or twenty days of experience, or are in roles that are permanent, temporary, or contract. Nobody should feel that their contribution is worth less than that of anyone else, no matter how menial or basic their work might be. If their contribution plays any part in the team's success, it's as important a contribution as any other. And if the work doesn't contribute to the team's success, why does the job exist at all?

You can get a good sense of how somebody perceives the value of their role—the meaning they find in their work—from their answer to the question, "What do you do?" If they answer something like, "I *just* clean the office," or "I'm *just* a cashier," or "I'm *only* a part-timer," that's a clear signal that this person feels much less valued in their role than you need them to feel.

Why does this matter? Because your team can only be as strong as its weakest link. Employees who feel that their contribution hardly matters engage less and contribute less than they could, leaving everyone worse off. It's in everybody's interest to ensure that people who earn less or occupy junior positions are engaged in your team and its activities to the same degree as others in higher-status positions.

Every employee should feel that their work adds value, is meaningful, and makes a difference in the lives of others. An engineer sinking a well in a deprived and drought-prone area would probably feel that their work matters. But if the same engineer had a job maintaining the production line in a soft-drink factory they might not feel the same and, if asked, might say that they "*just* make fizzy drinks." Like the latter engineer, most of us work in "ordinary" workplaces doing "ordinary" jobs that we can't really describe as meaningful. Fortunately, doing meaningful work is not the same as finding meaning at work. People *do* meaningful work, by, for example, serving a cause dear to their hearts. People *find* meaning at work by considering the value they add by doing what they do.

If work isn't intrinsically meaningful, you can't make it so, but you *can* help each employee find meaning in whatever job they are doing and in every workplace. Here's how:

- *Foster a sense of community.* People care about their work and their colleagues, and draw inspiration from that caring. Help your employees see how their contributions affect their workplace community. So, you'll get: "We just make fizzy drinks . . . but my work on keeping that line going allows the five hundred people who work here to put food on their family's table every day."

- *Give your employees autonomy.* Employees with a high level of freedom and discretion who feel that they are using their talents to realize their full potential are more likely to find meaning in their jobs. Our soft-drink engineer might then say: "It just produces fizzy drinks, but I'm proud to say that I've kept that production line going for the last seven years without a single breakdown."

- *Help employees feel pride in what they do and who they do it for.* Employees of well-respected organizations or well-loved brands will often find meaning in being part of that success. Remind employees of the value of their contribution to the overall success and brand of your company. Our engineer might say with pride: "I don't make fizzy drinks. I make Coca-Cola."

- *Let them know they belong.* Encourage *everyone* to take part fully in work and social activities, especially employees who work night shifts or work remotely. Shift employees often feel isolated. Remote workers often feel that others regard them as less committed and less hardworking than their colleagues based at headquarters, even though evidence shows that they tend to work longer—but different—hours and are often more productive because they suffer fewer distractions. Find ways to embrace them: invite them into the office or visit them regularly and include a social component in those meetings. Also, check in with them often by phone.

My client Dave operates about one hundred parking lots of varying sizes around Ireland. His employees work long hours, often alone in small huts or offices, and in all types of weather. He makes at least four visits to each location every year, requiring him to spend endless hours on the road. To stay connected to each of his spread-out employees, he calls them while driving, just to chat. His rule, which is strictly enforced, is that they can talk about anything at all *except* business matters—family, football, politics, the weather.

Dave's company was twice recognized as the Best Workplace in Ireland. It takes commitment and energy to make all those calls, but with every one, he helps his employees feel like they belong, that their jobs matter, that *they* matter and are trusted, and that they work for a company—and a boss—worth working for.

KEY POINTS

○ Never miss an opportunity to help employees understand how their efforts contribute to the success of the rest of the organization.

○ Let your employees have a say in how they do their jobs so they can take pride in their work and the talent they bring to it.

○ Include *everyone* in social and work activities so they feel part of your "family."

RULE 11

SHOW YOUR APPRECIATION

MOST OF US WORK HARD, most of the time. We work to the best of our ability, often putting in extra effort when we see that it's needed. Mostly, we just do what we do, quietly and without fuss. And although we don't need or expect constant praise or gratitude, it's nice when it happens.

Unfortunately, few of us are thanked or praised often enough or well enough. When is the last time an employee asked you to thank them less often, or to ease off on the praise? Precisely! And I doubt you've ever felt the need to make a similar request to *your* boss either.

Recognition is simply making others feel valued and appreciated for their work. It's important, and it's important to do it right. As is so often the case when managing people, it's not what you do, but how you do it, that makes the difference. Author and recognition expert Cindy Ventrice explains in her bestselling classic, *Make Their Day! Employee Recognition That Works,* "Recognition isn't a plaque; it's the meaning behind the plaque. It's about building relationships and taking a genuine personal interest in people and their preferences."[11]

Although we often talk about "recognition" and "rewards" in the same breath, they are quite different concepts. Both are given in exchange for good performance or effort and are intended to motivate employees individually and collectively. But while rewards usually cost money and offer a tangible benefit such as cash, a voucher, or an experience, the benefits of recognition are mainly psychological.

So, while rewards usually make us feel *good,* sincere, thoughtful, and well-executed recognition will always make us feel *great*! Best of all, although you're probably subject to some limits on how you reward your employees—because of budget or internal rules, for example—you get to call all the shots when it comes to recognition.

Because good recognition costs nothing but your time, thought, and effort.

BECOME A RECOGNITION BLACK BELT

Great recognition starts with great observation. To recognize good work, you've got to either see it personally or hear about it from someone else, and that means being present, connecting frequently with each of your employees, and showing interest in what they do. Be aware of the efforts and sacrifices that each of your people are making. Know who shows their devotion and dedication by regularly going above and beyond. Keep score. Remember, high-trust managers treat everyone *fairly*. They don't treat everyone the *same*.

Employees so rarely receive personal attention from their leaders that, when it happens, they notice. That's why recognition works. So, make it happen. Recognize any behaviors that exceed expectations. Recognize outstanding contributions, but also recognize the many "little things" that make the difference, such as a job well done, a helping hand, or perfect attendance.

Never show recognition when it's not deserved. To be effective, praise must be selective. If you praise everyone and everything your praise will soon mean nothing. A good rule of thumb is that if you can't be clear and *specific* about the behavior or attitude that made the achievement possible, it's probably not a good idea to celebrate it.

Praise is a powerful tool for managers, and while generic praise is probably better than none, the most effective praise is specific to the employee's behavior or performance. When recognizing someone's work, talk less about *what* was achieved and focus instead on *how* it was achieved. For example, don't just praise an employee for being a "great team member," praise them for "demonstrating great teamwork by staying late with Mark and Martha to help them with an urgent client request." This shows employees that you appreciate them working the right way, even if it doesn't always lead to the desired results.

Never mix praise and feedback in the same conversation. Your employee will only hear the feedback. Or criticism. "You showed great patience and kindness in helping that client" is praise. "But next time you might also consider . . ." is coaching. Praise now. Save coaching for later.

Tailor how you recognize each individual to prevent your well-intentioned gestures from backfiring. Although giving appropriate recognition is an invaluable motivational tool, one size does not fit all. Yes, everybody likes to feel appreciated, but not everybody likes to be appreciated *in the same way*. Different employees will receive identical gestures differently, depending on their personality and their relationship with you. Some employees, for example, thrive on public recognition and praise, while others would want to curl up and die if singled out for public acknowledgment.

Recognition doesn't have to be big and pricey to be memorable and meaningful. Most of the time, free and simple works best. Offer your recognition with sincerity and offer it regularly. This shows your employees that you value them. Your praise is—without exaggeration—powerful enough to change lives! Maya Angelou, the American poet and civil rights activist, understood this when she said, "I've learned that people will forget what you said, people will forget what you did, but people will never forget how you made them feel."

While recognizing an individual's contributions underpins their strong performance and increases their morale, *team* recognition is also important and effective. Your challenge is to strike a balance between the two. If you focus too much on individual performance, you'll undermine teamwork and create an overly competitive environment, and your employees will believe that this is what you value most. If you reward teams without acknowledging individual contributions, you risk demoralizing your high achievers, leaving them wondering why they bother to work so hard when everybody gets to share in the praise. The solution? Recognize both team and individual performance, while being sure to promote and reward "cooperation" as a valued behavior.

Also, remember to show appreciation for those who are moving on, whether they are leaving through retirement or to pursue new paths. Taking the opportunity to say thank you for their contributions is reason enough to do it, but in doing so you also show everyone else on the team how they can expect to be treated when it comes time for *them* to move on. A manager who ignores or barely recognizes a departing colleague's contributions sends a clear message to everyone else that, when their time comes, they can expect little thanks for past efforts and achievements. On the flip side, sincere and thoughtful recognition sends a message of value and appreciation, not just to that departing employee, but to everyone.

THE BEST THINGS IN LIFE ARE (OFTEN) FREE

When it comes to recognition, it's often the thought that counts. No budget for fancy Christmas gifts? Hot chocolate and doughnuts on a cold Monday afternoon in late January will be more appreciated and make a greater impact than anything else you could offer in the weeks before Christmas, when gifts are commonplace. Consider what other gifts are at your disposal and within your authority: A few hours off. A late start. An early finish. A day off. Use of your parking space. A day in your comfortable chair. Whatever. The gift itself is far less important than the recognition that the gift confers.

Here's a small selection of recognition ideas that you can implement at little or no cost, and without anybody else's approval:

- *Say thank you.* Drop by the employee's work space to tell them how much you appreciate their extra effort.

- *Write a note.* Show your appreciation by writing a personal thank-you e-mail, card, or, for even more impact, a handwritten letter.

- *Share employees' successes with the entire team.* When an employee receives positive customer feedback or you receive an e-mail complimenting a member of your team for a job well done, don't keep it to yourself. Circulate the e-mail to everyone on the team, share the feedback at a regular team meeting, or display it on a "thank you" notice board.

- *Praise during team meetings.* Plan time during team meetings to recognize and thank employees who have gone above and beyond. But don't praise for the sake of it. If you thank too many people too often, soon no one will notice anymore. When you have nothing worth saying, say nothing.

- *Take the employee out to lunch.* Don't worry if you have a limited budget. Most employees won't care about the venue or expense; they value that you've singled them out and made time to spend with them.

- *Pay for the employee to enjoy dinner on you.* Some employees would enjoy an all-expenses-paid meal with their boss; others would prefer to enjoy the treat with their partner.

- *Throw an ad hoc informal celebration.* Grab a cake or a bag of fruit or candy, then gather your team and explain why you've invited them to this small celebration. Or arrange a celebratory lunch or picnic. Better still, when you're showing appreciation for an individual employee, ask their closest friend at the company to organize the celebration so they can come up with more personalized and creative ideas.

- *Celebrate employee birthdays.* Or work anniversaries. Or both. There's no shortage of events to mark—the birth of a child or a grandchild or even the birth of puppies or kittens. Remember that the reason for the celebration is to show your appreciation of who the employee is and what they bring to the team. The event itself is just a hook on which to hang your appreciation.

- *Hold an employee-appreciation week.* You are limited only by your budget and your imagination, in that order. Low-cost celebrations and sincere, well-chosen words will make a much greater impact than big, showy gestures and vague platitudes.

- *Share your recognition with the employee's family.* Some managers like to drop a note to the employee's family, highlighting the employee's valuable contributions to the team. But only do so if you are familiar with the employee's family circumstances. While it can be a highly effective recognition tool, it also carries potential for disaster. A note from you to an employee's family, acknowledging the gargantuan effort and extra hours that the employee worked during the last six months, could prove to be the last straw in their relationship if their absences from home have been a cause of ongoing friction.

• *Host an annual awards ceremony for your team.* Let your team explore their creative side and plan whatever they come up with. Present a mix of individual and team award categories—some serious, some less so. A framed certificate for each award is all that you need, or how about custom-made awards that relate in a unique way to the work that your team does? You're not trying to compete with the Oscars and it really *is* the thought that counts. When you open the ceremony, take a few minutes to highlight the team-building behaviors that are being celebrated, but don't belabor the point. The recognition is important, but so is the shared team experience and enjoyment—so aim for plenty of laughter and lots of fun!

• *Encourage peers to recognize each other.* Employees get a boost from knowing that their colleagues appreciate the contributions that they make. Peer recognition works best when it's driven by the team. If you're seen to be the one who is pushing it, there's a danger that your employees will come to regard it as just another management tool. Float the idea of a peer-recognition program to your team, then get out of the way. Let them decide how they'd like to do it—formal, informal, or a combination of both. Any approach will do, so long as it achieves the desired outcomes.

TOO BUSY FOR THANKS? THINK AGAIN!

The high-trust manager makes appreciation a priority. Don't fall into the trap of believing you don't have time to do it. You might as well say that you don't have time to manage. A little and often works best, because timing is everything. Don't wait six months until it's time for the official performance review. When you see or hear about good performance, acknowledge it! Even when you're busy, don't leave recognition for later. Your job becomes easier, not harder, when you invest the time and effort to recognize your employees' efforts and achievements.

KEY POINTS

○ It's almost impossible to thank or praise too much. Remember, when it comes to recognition, "free, simple, and often" is the way to go.

○ Don't just tell an employee they did a great job; tell them *how* they did a great job.

○ Never praise for the sake of praising. Everyone sees through it, and it reduces the impact of the sincere praise that you offer at other times.

GET TO KNOW THE WHOLE PERSON

YOU HAVE A LIFE OUTSIDE the company and so does every member of your team. Just as most of an iceberg lies hidden beneath the surface, what you see of each employee in the workplace is only a tiny part of that person and their life. There are many other aspects of life that are—or should be—of greater importance than their jobs: family, pets, and hobbies, for example.

Each of us is a unique and special individual, with a past, present, and future separate from, and independent of, our day-to-day work persona. Each of us has our beliefs and values. Most have responsibilities to family, friends, and neighbors. Some play central roles in clubs, societies, churches, and communities. Others are pet lovers, mountain climbers, jigsaw-puzzle buffs, or amateur historians. Most of us are defined much more by our personal circumstances, responsibilities, and interests than we are by what we do for a living.

When you show a sincere interest in your team members as unique individuals and not just as employees, you show respect for the complexities of their lives. In doing so, you prepare the ground for them to trust you and your sincerity on other occasions.

Showing interest in your employees' personal lives doesn't require any intrusive behavior or questions on your part. Some employees guard their privacy carefully and keep clear barriers between their work and personal lives. Others see little distinction between the two and are happy to share each with people whom they trust. In the same way, some managers have a natural flair for putting people at ease by chatting about personal matters, while others find it excruciatingly difficult. The key is to find the middle ground on which both you and your employee feel comfortable and where each of you can be fully "yourself."

Your role as a caring manager is simply to show by your words and actions that you understand that each of

your colleagues is much more than "just an employee."
It's less about knowing the minute details of what's going
on in your employee's life and more about showing your
understanding that whatever is happening in their life is
important to them and is to be respected.

Here are some ideas for how you can appreciate and
respect the individuality of each member of your team:

- *Whenever you greet or talk to employees, use their
  names.* It's a simple yet powerful way to show that
  you recognize them as a unique individual. If you
  don't know their name, find out.

- *Drop by the desks of employees who just came back
  from vacation.* Ask them about their time off and
  bring them up to date on any news—social and
  professional—they might have missed.

- *Check on a sick employee.* When an employee is ill
  at home, call to ask how they're doing and if they
  need any help. Do not, under any circumstances,
  discuss anything work related on this call. Your
  employee might think that the work issue—and
  not their welfare—was the primary reason for your
  call. If you need to discuss work matters, and it's
  appropriate to do so, make a separate call.

- *Connect with an employee who returns from being out sick.* Ask about their health without being intrusive and let them know about anything that happened in their absence, particularly non-work-related happenings or news.

- *Call employees who work remotely.* From time to time, reach out to employees who work from home or in other locations, just to see how they're doing.

- *Show empathy for employees going through a challenging time.* Whether they are planning a wedding or expecting a baby, or are dealing with the death or illness of a close family member, they need your understanding and compassion. Do whatever you can to accommodate them. Some may just need to be cut some slack, some might need a little flexibility around their schedule, and others might need temporary concessions, such as permission (and privacy) to make or take personal calls at work.

- *Really listen to what people tell you about their personal lives.* The simple act of showing employees that you have heard them and remember what they shared with you demonstrates that you care. Whether it's remembering to ask how an employee's child performed in their school play, or sympathizing when the sports team an employee fanatically supports loses, act on what they chose to share with you.

- *Host lunchtime information sessions on topics that relate to employees' personal lives.* Outside experts are usually happy to conduct sessions free of charge on issues like retirement planning, nutrition, parenting, and the like as it raises their profile and can lead to future sales or referrals. Or tap into the expertise of your employees. How about brown-bag lunches to share their hobbies or passions—whether it's quilting, chess, or genealogy—with their peers?

- *Encourage employees to decorate their personal work space.* Lead by example and inspire them to show off their photographs and other personal items, such as their kids' drawings, vacation souvenirs, and, of course, the many treasured praise notes, thank-you cards, and certificates that you and their colleagues—inspired by Rule 11—have given them in recent months!

- *Make full use of any company-wide social events.*
  These might include family days, or bring-your-
  kid-to-work or bring-your-pet-to-work days. On
  your own, you might be able to arrange a team
  barbecue or movie outing that includes your
  employees' families or spouses.

Each of these strategies will allow you to become
closer to your employees. But an important word of
caution: as you get to know the person you might learn
intimate details of that person's life. You must keep confidential *everything* that an employee chooses to share
with you.

It might seem obvious that you shouldn't share any
health-related information or any personal financial
issues that you become aware of. But you can't assume
that it's OK to share anything else that an employee tells
you with anybody else. If they want others on the team
to know where they're going on vacation, or that their
daughter's cat is ill, or that their partner has joined a
choir, they will tell them themselves. By sharing nuggets
of others' news or information, you don't so much risk
betraying confidentiality as you risk becoming known
as a gossip. And that would be hugely damaging to your
efforts to build trust.

Figure out which of the strategies above works best for your team, but remember, as always in great workplaces, it's not about *what* you do but *how* and *why* you do it. Remember that there is much more to each of your team members than what you see in the workplace. Show sincere interest in getting to know everyone on your team, respect each person's individuality, and embrace and celebrate the many differences that together make your workplace—and the people who work in it—so special. Everything else will fall into place.

KEY POINTS

○ Each employee's personal life involves worry and joy, stress and laughter—just like yours. Respect and support each employee in the way that you'd like *your manager* to respect and support you.

○ Show by your words and actions that each of your colleagues is much more than "just an employee."

○ Keep confidential everything that an employee chooses to share with you. *Everything*.

HELP YOUR EMPLOYEES ACHIEVE WORK-LIFE BALANCE

WORK AFFECTS THE PERSONAL LIFE of every employee on your team, and their personal lives affect their work. High-trust managers show respect for the whole person by helping them to balance these often-conflicting responsibilities. Doing so lessens the likelihood of burnout and leads to a more vital and interesting group of employees who are energized by activities outside the workplace and able to focus better when at work.

Your challenge is to help each employee to achieve the balance that works best for them. Since each employee is an individual with unique needs and personal circumstances, a one-size-fits-all approach won't work.

When it comes to work-life balance, managers fall into three distinct camps. There are those who believe that it's vitally important for everyone, those who believe that it's for wimps, and those who are somewhere in between. It's important for you to know where you stand, because in my experience, managers' attitudes toward helping their employees achieve work-life balance tend to reflect their personal approach to work-life balance.

In other words, if you work eighteen hours a day and think work-life balance is only for losers, you are unlikely to put much effort into helping your team achieve that balance. Similarly, if it's important for you to get home most evenings to feed your cat, or to attend choir rehearsal, or to read your kids their bedtime story, you are likely to also support your colleagues' efforts to achieve balance between work and other priorities.

Personally, I place a high value on work-life balance, partly because I believe that there's a lot more to life than work, and partly because I believe that we each work best when we get to enjoy reasonable downtime. It's hard to sustain great effort when one long month rolls into another and then another. I recognize, though, that some employers demand long hours and that some employees are happy to work those hours. What's important is that as a manager you help each of your employees achieve the level of balance in their lives that *they* feel is reasonable. Problems arise only when there's a bad fit between what we feel is reasonable and what can be achieved.

Get a clear understanding of what each individual employee is striving for, explain what you or the organization need from that employee, and discuss any gap or mismatch in expectations. While the benefits of a good work-life balance may seem obvious, it's not easily achieved in every job, nor does everyone strive to work eight hours daily and no more. It all comes down to the "bargain" you strike with your employee.

A few years ago, I worked with a client—a recruitment firm—whose employees rated it very highly in every area except work-life balance. When I asked employees at the firm whether management *encouraged* them to balance their work life and their personal life, most employees responded "sometimes yes and sometimes no."

I expressed my concern to the owner of the firm, but he shared a different perspective. Long hours and high pay are a feature of this job, he explained. "Our recruiters must start each day early and finish late to meet with job seekers outside of normal office hours," he said. "And in between, they work hard to place those people in suitable jobs. We make it very clear when we interview them and at all other stages of the recruitment process that a sixty-hour week is the norm. Most recruiters work with us for about seven years and earn a small fortune before leaving us for a more regular job in a human resources function within another company—at lower pay, of course."

My later work with that client allowed me to get to know many of his staff, and I found that what he had told me was true. All new hires were made aware of the realities of their new job: that they could expect to earn above-average pay for working above-average hours. When a recruiter's personal life became more important than a large paycheck, they moved on or moved up. My mistake was in failing to appreciate that although my client's employees had told me they were not *encouraged* to balance their work and personal lives, they had not suggested that they were *unhappy* about that.

Incidentally, thanks mainly to its employees' input, that recruitment firm was later recognized by Great Place to Work as the #1 Best Workplace in its country. This honor proves that a requirement to work long and unsociable hours is no barrier to building a high-trust workplace if the organization is clear and truthful in setting expectations and gives everyone a fair share of the rewards earned through those long hours.

Just as not all jobs facilitate good work-life balance, not all employees strive for a regular forty-hour, five-day week. Many of us will willingly put in extra hours on an exciting project, or to meet an important deadline, or to respond to an emergency or unusual opportunity. Employees just starting out in their careers will often happily invest long hours for a variety of reasons: to learn the work better, to earn more money, to make a good impression, or for the sheer enjoyment and sense of purpose they get from working on a stimulating project. At other times, employees may want to reduce the hours they work to allow more time for other things that they find important.

So how can a high-trust manager reconcile the need to achieve results (the reason the organization exists in the first place) with the desire to help employees achieve a reasonable work-life balance?

First, draw a clear distinction—and be sure that everyone understands the difference—between core requirements and discretionary effort. The former is mandatory and the least that you expect of an employee to perform the job. In other words, that *is the job*. Discretionary effort involves going the extra mile, doing more than is needed to perform the core requirements of the job.

No employee should feel pressured or coerced into regularly working extra hours. But most jobs might need employees to occasionally work harder and longer hours, for example to meet a production deadline or seasonal demand. And most employees will be happy to play their part if this surge in expectations is limited. It's important to respect the circumstances of those employees who can't make a significant discretionary effort, and it's equally important to recognize and reward those who do make the extra effort. It's the difference between feeling exploited and feeling appreciated.

Second, make sure employees don't work too hard simply to make a good impression. One of the biggest challenges around work-life balance is that when you have ambitious people working in dynamic organizations, there will always be a tendency for employees to try to impress you by working long hours, or at least by being present at their desks for long hours. While these tendencies may lead to short-term advantages for your team, the benefits will be eliminated by longer-term issues, such as burnout, illness, absenteeism, high employee turnover, low-quality work, and poor team morale.

There are many ways to discourage your employees from overextending themselves at work. To show your genuine respect for the personal responsibilities of your team, try to avoid scheduling early-morning and late-evening meetings. While such meetings are convenient for some employees and can be highly productive, they can pose challenges for parents, caregivers, and employees who are involved in activities with inflexible schedules, like volunteering or taking classes. This is particularly the case when you call such meetings on short or no notice. If you can't avoid early or late meetings, try to schedule them well in advance and be sure to finish them by the scheduled time.

Like many managers, you may choose to send and respond to e-mails outside of official work hours. There's nothing wrong with this practice if everyone understands why you do it. Explain to your team that it suits your work patterns, but you don't expect them to check or respond to e-mails outside of official work hours. Many employees worry that if they don't check their e-mail outside regular business hours, they may miss an important or urgent request from their boss. One way to allay any such fears is to promise to call them if anything urgent comes up.

Third, make sure your employees are comfortable asking for time off from work to take care of unforeseen personal needs. Great Place to Work research suggests that, since the responsibility for responding to family emergencies still falls overwhelmingly on women, they often seek such flexibility more often than men. Thus, they are less confident about asking for flexible accommodations when confronted with unexpected circumstances.

Fourth, be fair. Work-life balance is not only about helping parents strike a balance between their work and family responsibilities. Not every employee has children and those employees are no less deserving of your support in achieving a satisfactory work-life balance. If you consistently prioritize accommodating employees with children at the expense of those without, resentment can often arise. As one employee told me, "I'm happy for mothers and fathers to achieve work-life balance. But is it fair that it's always me that is asked to come in early or stay late or work weekends, just because I don't have kids?"

Grandparents can have child-care responsibilities. And employees are often responsible for their aging parents or even siblings. For some employees, a sick dog or cat is—understandably—as big a worry and as significant a problem as a sick child is for others. Good work-life balance is a legitimate ambition for everyone. Taking the time to learn about each of your employees' lives will help you to accommodate their unique circumstances.

A few years ago, PepsiCo launched an initiative to help employees sustain their work-life balance called "One Simple Thing." As part of the program, managers ask each of their staff, "What one simple thing would be of greatest help to you in supporting your work-life balance?" Some employees decide, for example, that leaving the office at a specific time is the "one thing" for them. Others prioritize engaging in regular exercise or committing to "e-mail-free" weekends and holidays. Still others value most being available to pick up their kids from school, learning a new skill, or simply taking time out for themselves. Once an employee has decided their "one thing," their manager documents and checks their progress and can even reward employees who stick to their plan, as part of the annual performance-review process.

This initiative works on so many levels. It recognizes that one size does not fit all and requires a commitment on the part of the manager to find good, individualized solutions for each employee. But it's also about partnership. It's not left only to the manager to "fix" their employees' work-life balance, but neither is it solely the responsibility of the individual employee to figure out how to accomplish that balance. Instead, both work together to find a great solution that works for everyone.

Although PepsiCo's One Simple Thing is an organization-wide initiative, you could probably introduce a similar program for your team, because, in most cases, the "one thing" that employees need is flexibility in their schedule or work duties, which most managers have the authority to accommodate.

Perhaps the most effective way in which you can support your team in achieving work-life balance is to lead by example. One professional-services organization introduced a "Summer Fridays" initiative that allowed employees to complete five days' work in four and a half days, then leave the office at one o'clock on Fridays throughout the summer. On the first Friday of the summer, most employees stayed through the afternoon, even though they had worked the longer hours the previous four days. The HR department realized that few leaders—partners and senior managers—had left early, so employees felt it would look bad if they left while their bosses continued working. The following Friday, the HR department encouraged bosses to leave at one o'clock, sending a clear message to everyone else that it was acceptable to start the weekend early. It worked.

When you show by your actions that you are serious about your career and committed to having a satisfying personal life, you effectively give permission to your employees to do the same.

KEY POINTS

○ Actively encourage employees to make full
use of the benefits your company offers,
such as childcare leave.

○ Some jobs and industries are, by design,
not as flexible when it comes to helping
employees achieve work-life balance. If your
team falls in this category, be explicit about
it with your employees during the hiring
process so they know what to expect.

○ Work-life balance is necessary for everyone—
not just employees with children. Make sure
all your employees feel comfortable asking
you for flexibility with their schedules when
unexpected personal circumstances demand
it of them.

RULE 14

Treat Everyone Fairly

Treating your employees fairly is not the same as treating them equally. Treating employees *equally* means treating everyone the same; treating your employees *fairly* means treating each employee in a way that is appropriate to the contribution that they make. Even if they have the same role, no two employees are alike. They might have different work styles, skill sets, personal responsibilities, and goals, and therefore get the job done in very different ways and contribute at different levels.

The justification for treating everyone fairly is simple—it's the right thing to do! And the benefits are many.

Treating people fairly accommodates and encourages diversity within the organization. A fair work environment reduces the distractions of inequity, politics, and prejudice, and allows everyone to make their greatest contributions.

Treating everyone fairly means a complete absence of discrimination on any grounds, including gender, gender identity, physical abilities, religion, sexual orientation, weight, or any other personal characteristic. Thankfully, many countries have legislation that makes it unlawful to discriminate on such grounds, and most organizations want to keep on the right side of the law.

And yet, often, the reason we don't treat everyone fairly is because, despite our belief that we don't discriminate, our biases get the best of us. What's the difference between bias and discrimination? Let's take gender as an example. If a friend tells you that the nurse at the hospital did a great job dressing their wound, you might imagine that the nurse is female. That's gender bias, because you presumed that the job of a nurse would be done by a female worker. But if you are the patient and refuse to let a male nurse dress your wounds, that's gender discrimination.

It's a safe bet that you, like most decent people, believe you would never discriminate against any employee. But you do. We all do. Every day we make snap judgments and assessments of people and situations based on stereotypes and misinformation shaped through our background, cultural environment, and experiences. We categorize and judge people before we even realize it's happening, which is why these attitudes are called unconscious biases.

These biases can work to the advantage of some people, while others suffer because of them. For example, we place certain values on people based on their age. We often credit younger workers as having more energy, motivation, and ability to learn—and believe them to be more unreliable, likely to call in sick even if they are not ill, or to leave to "go find themselves" on the other side of the world. Many managers see mature employees as more experienced and reliable—and also set in their ways and slow to adapt. Of course, these judgments may or may not be true. Every person younger or older is different.

To our shame, we project values and attitudes on people based not only on the "usual" grounds such as age or gender, but also on their name, where they live, what they wear, whether they are an introvert or an extrovert, and even the music they like. And the list of unconscious biases that society has toward people with disabilities could fill a book on its own.

Before you defend yourself by saying that although you understand how *others* might discriminate in this way, you never would . . . don't bother. That's what everyone says! There's even a name for it: blind-spot bias, whereby we recognize the impact of biases on the judgment of others, while not seeing the impact of biases on our own judgment.

How do you overcome unconscious bias? The somewhat trite answer is, "With great difficulty." Our biases are deeply ingrained and are more a reflection of how our brains work and the power of our subconscious minds than of our values or the respect that we have for others. That's why self-awareness is your most effective weapon against your unconscious biases. Be aware of the problem and accept that it's there, even if you don't see it in yourself. Be alert for it. When you find yourself projecting any value—negative or otherwise—onto anyone, stop and ask yourself, "How do I know this to be true?" Unless you have solid facts to support an assumption, discard it.

Sometimes we show a bias in favor of people who are "like us." That is, people we warm more quickly to or better understand. Or people we have more in common with—people with kids, no kids, pets, a love of travel— or were friends with before we became managers. And sometimes this bias leads to favoritism, which can then manifest itself in the business decisions we make, such as allocating shifts or better assignments—or in what is, for many employees, the litmus test for fairness in the workplace: the promotion process.

Generally, employees put themselves forward for a promotion because they believe that they deserve it. And it hurts badly when they don't get it. They want to understand why they were rejected and they look around for someone or something to blame. The *someone* is usually either the person who got the promotion or the person who gave it to them, or both. And the natural tendency is for the employee to see the *something* as a bias against them or in favor of someone else.

Be scrupulously fair when selecting employees for promotion, and communicate clearly the reasons why you promoted the successful candidate. Otherwise, people will fall back on the easy excuse: you play golf with them, you lunch with them, your kids are in the same school, you are neighbors, whatever. This reaction is understandable. It comes from disappointment, and when we are disappointed, we often look beyond ourselves for reasons to explain our setbacks.

When you promote the best person, you reward individual talent and effort, boost team morale, and enhance your reputation as a competent and fair manager. Putting anybody but the best person into any position will cost you dearly in terms of the damage and upset caused to the passed-over employee—to say nothing of the impact on your team's morale, performance, and results, and the significant cost to your personal reputation. And if the promoted candidate knows deep down that they really weren't the best candidate, you won't even get *their* respect.

Most employees will accept being turned down for a promotion and feel that you have treated them fairly if you give them honest and constructive feedback. Why did they not earn it and how might they improve their performance to have a better chance next time? Your feedback should focus on reasons, reassurance, and if necessary, refocusing.

- *Reasons.* Why didn't the employee get the hoped-for promotion? Share those reasons honestly but sensitively. Discuss the skill set and experience that you needed in the position and, without betraying confidentiality, share the reasons why you promoted the person you did. Focus on the positive. Discuss the skills and attributes that the employee can develop rather than what they are lacking. Make sure that this meeting is a conversation, not a pronouncement. Simply telling them why they didn't get the promotion might seem easier, but it's better to help them see for themselves why they weren't ready for this move.

- *Reassurance.* Explain the contributions that this person brings to your team. Everyone wants to know that they are valued and that their contribution counts. Otherwise, why would they make anything but the minimum effort at work? Reassure them that they are a valued and valuable member of the team.

- *Refocusing.* If you believe that the employee has the potential to advance further on your team or in the wider organization in the future, say so. But if they've gone as far as they are likely to go on your team, it's time for them to refocus. If they are stuck in a career cul-de-sac, they deserve to know that. Although you can offer no further room for progression, maybe you see opportunities for them to advance outside of your team, or maybe outside of your organization. Talk about those opportunities. No single organization can offer unlimited advancement potential to everyone. Your employee may very well be ahead of you in figuring all this out because, deep down, most of us know our limitations. Sometimes we just need to hear the truth from someone else to spur us toward action.

Of course, perceptions of fairness start well before any promotion opportunity becomes available. Your responsibility is to manage each employee's expectation and development. Help those who can advance understand what they must do to advance. Help those who are not capable of advancing to explore whether they could be more successful elsewhere or in a different role. Each employee deserves equal support from you in figuring out their career direction.

Perceptions of unfairness in the promotion process matter, and they can cause an enthusiastic and committed employee to become disengaged and resentful. Worse, they can cause a whole team to switch off. But if employees believe the system is fair for everyone, they will enter the promotion "competition" with more confidence and less anxiety about the outcome, knowing that you will treat them fairly.

Finally, remember that the more of a track record of fairness you create in all your business decisions—not just promotions—the more confidence everyone around you will have in your objectivity, and the more likely they'll be to give you the benefit of the doubt when you

make a decision that has the potential to upset some of
your team.

KEY POINTS

○ Perceptions are reality. It's not enough to be fair; you must always be *seen* to be fair. To an employee, if it *seems* unfair, it *is* unfair.

○ Those who have the least relative power are more likely to suffer discrimination and less likely to have the confidence or the power to defend themselves or ask others to help them do so. Be vigilant for any signs of discrimination or unconscious bias and be ready to intervene to stamp it out.

○ It's easier to treat people equally than fairly. Be courageous and differentiate. As Thomas Jefferson reportedly said: "Nothing is more unequal than the equal treatment of unequal people."

RULE 15

DO WHAT YOU ARE PAID TO DO

BEING COMPETENT AT YOUR JOB is essential for creating trust with your employees. Your employees might like you, they might appreciate your intentions, and they might want to trust you, but they simply won't trust you if you can't do the job you're paid to do.

Your team must also *believe* that you are competent, and for that to happen, you must consistently show competence. It's only when your employees experience you as competent that they will be willing to trust your decisions and to follow you—especially when you are trying to lead them through times of change or uncertainty.

Each of your employees has an opinion about your competence, arrived at with little or no conscious thought. Their assessment encompasses everything that you do from before a new member joins the team to after they've left, and all points in between. Essentially, it comes down to a feeling. No evidence offered, no chance to mount a defense, no court of appeal. Nobody said management was easy!

Numerous books have been written about how to manage with competence, but here's a cheat-sheet summary: Develop a vision. Plan for success. And manage.

- *Develop a shared vision.* Draw on the values and vision of the organization to help create a clear sense of direction for your team. Listen. Ask for input from everyone on your team and carefully consider what they tell you. Listen more. Only shared visions inspire and command ongoing support.

- *Plan for success.* Deploy your team and resources effectively. The starting point is to know your team. Understand each person's strengths and weaknesses, and assign them responsibilities in a way that allows each of them to be challenged without being overwhelmed. There's a thin line between a manageable workload and an unmanageable one. A competent manager knows the difference.

- *Manage*. Ensure that each person on your team delivers. Expect competence from each of your employees and hold them accountable for the quality of their work. Your team won't thank you for making excuses for poor performance because that shifts the workload to them. If an employee isn't performing well, it could indicate an unreasonable workload, or a skills or training deficit, or a lack of interest or commitment, or a poor hiring decision. Maybe you didn't have any say in recruiting this person—inherited employees are a reality of almost every management position—but you're the manager now and therefore you're 100 percent responsible. So, find the underlying cause and take action. Be supportive, but performance is nonnegotiable.

If sometimes you're overwhelmed by what it takes to be a competent manager, you're not alone. Managing is a journey to competence, and we are all on that journey. Remember that the opposite of competent isn't always *in*competent. Sometimes, the opposite is *not* *competent* and there's a world of difference between the two. *Incompetent* implies abject failure—an inability to do the job—while *not competent* merely suggests that you're just not quite there *yet*. Stick with it. You don't need to be brilliant to be a great manager, because when it comes to competence, "good enough" *is* good enough.

KEY POINTS

○ Develop a shared-vision plan for your team by asking for their input.

○ Deploy your team effectively: allow each member to feel challenged without being overwhelmed.

○ Hold your employees accountable for their competence. Be supportive, but ensure each person delivers.

RULE 16

HAVE FUN
TOGETHER

YOUR BOSS IS A NASTY person.

They lie to you and don't keep even their smallest promises. Just last week, you heard through the grapevine that they have passed you over for a promotion that you worked hard to earn and that *everybody* knows you deserved. And they haven't even had the courtesy to tell you to your face yet. No wonder you distrust them intensely. As do most of your colleagues.

But everything might be about to change. Your boss has a plan. They have designated today as "Weird 'n' Wacky Wednesday," an initiative they described in an e-mail to the group as "a zany, super crazy, anything-goes fun day." They hope it will boost morale and help the team to bond better.

Now it's 9:05 a.m. on Wednesday. You're already at work and deep in concentration, having come in early this morning to finish a time-sensitive proposal. You sense the person standing near your desk more than you see them—a multicolored clown standing over you, a grotesque ear-to-ear smile on their chalk-white face. They tickle your chin with a brightly colored feather duster as they inhale deeply from the helium tank resting on the floor beside them. "Go Tea-m, Go Tea-m!" they squeak manically over and over and over again as they take aim, soaking your work with their trick water-squirting sunflower.

Wacky!

Are you having fun yet?

Managers everywhere struggle to wrap their heads around the concept of "fun at work." Some dismiss it as childish, silly, unprofessional, and a waste of time, making comments such as, "People are here to work; we're not running a kindergarten." Others fear that it will get out of hand.

But when it comes to fun at work, nothing could be further from the truth.

Fun at work is simply *the freedom to be yourself at work*. It's knowing that your colleagues accept you as you are and you accepting your colleagues on the same terms. It's laughter when we're happy and consolation when we face a setback. It's joy when we're celebrating and a way to let off steam on bad days. It relieves boredom at quiet times and offers a safety valve when we're under pressure. It builds team spirit, and it reveals the spirit that's already there. Fun is fun when you're with people you like.

Fun at work is an essential element of all great workplaces and highly correlated to trust. When you come across workers having genuine fun in the workplace you know that you've found a high-trust team. Employees who strongly agree that they have fun at work are also extremely likely to strongly agree that, taking everything into account, theirs is a great place to work. There is also a similar correlation between fun and effective recruiting, employee turnover, and camaraderie or teamwork. Although we know for certain that fun and trust are closely correlated, the data doesn't prove if having fun causes high trust, or if high trust causes or enables the fun to happen.

In my experience, it's a bit of both.

Fun doesn't build trust—at least, not in any significant way. Fun happens because of the trust that's already there. But fun *reinforces* trust because it reinforces the bonds of the team. It signals that we are comfortable with each other, that we get along, that we can take a few minutes to enjoy ourselves without fear of being judged or criticized. You don't get that freedom in a low-trust workplace.

Fun means different things to different people, and fun at work is no different. Similarly, the appetite for fun varies from one person to another, so high-trust managers find ways to have fun at work that are right for individual employees, their team, and their organization. The type of industry or business sector influences how and when employees have fun. For example, funeral directors might be more restrained in how they have fun at work than employees in, say, a microbrewery or a tech start-up.

The age profile of your team makes a difference too. Research reported by Businessinsider.com found that although almost 90 percent of younger workers want to have a "fun and social work environment," only 60 percent of employees over 50 want the same.[12] The same research found that 71 percent of younger workers want their coworkers to be their "second family." But older workers, many of whom go home to their "first families" at the end of each day and have better-established social lives, may prefer to keep their personal and professional lives separate. After-work bowling is a hoot when you've nothing special to do and all evening to do it. But maybe it loses its appeal when set against the chance to tuck your kids in after you read them their bedtime story.

Here are some ideas and practical insights that will help you foster a sense of fun in your workplace:

- *Let it happen.* It's OK to plan events that you hope will be fun, but we find some of the best fun at work in routine day-to-day activities. A witty comment. A funny story, spontaneously told. Calling a colleague the wrong name or getting your words mixed up. Shared memories and shared photos. Simple fun. Let it happen by showing that, when it happens, you're OK with that.

- *Lead by example.* Show that you're happy for your team to enjoy fun at work by joining in. Smile. Disapproval can be communicated nonverbally, as can approval. Better, lead the way and start the fun from time to time if you can do so authentically. But if it doesn't come naturally to you, don't try to fake it. You can't fake fun.

- *Teach* when *to have fun.* A great place to work is primarily a place to *work*. Fun at work is a delicate balance between doing the work that you are paid to do and having fun while doing it. Not everyone will instinctively grasp that it's about work first, fun second. Sometimes, and for understandable reasons, younger and less-experienced employees can struggle to strike the right balance between work and play. Help them to develop greater awareness of when to play and when to keep their heads down, coaching discreetly just as you would in any other area of performance.

- *Set the limits.* It's important to have boundaries. The unacceptable is never acceptable, even in the name of fun. *Especially* in the name of fun. Whether it's a joke or a casual remark or a comment in office banter, good taste and accepted norms must apply. Fun is only fun if it's fun for everyone involved. Adopt a zero-tolerance approach, but be sensitive. A quiet word will often be enough to keep things in check.

- *Schedule events, not "fun."* When you arrange to meet your friends for a Sunday brunch, you write it in your calendar as "Brunch." You expect to have fun, but you don't write it in as "Fun." (*Tell* me you don't!) It's the same at work. Schedule coffee and doughnuts for Monday morning and it will almost certainly be a fun activity. Lighthearted banter, catching up, a sugar rush and a caffeine hit, making plans, laughing together. But invite your team to a "Fun & Doughnuts Event" and you'll probably get to eat alone. Nothing scares normal people quite as much as organized fun.

- *Have fun with a purpose.* Do something good as a team and have fun doing it. Volunteer. Pack groceries for charity. Paint a school. Go carol singing or join a fund-raising walk or start a communal effort to get into better shape. Clear litter from a stretch of coast or help out at a homeless shelter. Have fun. Do good.

- *Mix it up.* One size doesn't fit all. The more diverse your team, the greater the challenge of finding activities that make work fun for everyone. Ask for ideas and see what works. Experiment. See how different people respond to different activities and tailor future events accordingly. It's not necessary for every employee to take part in every activity, but don't allow your team to split into permanent groups that only ever socialize together—for example, younger workers in one camp, older workers in the other. Social groupings can morph into workplace cliques and that's not good for teamwork or unity.

Workplace fun is an attitude, a state of mind that allows people to connect and affirm their common bonds. Many of your employees spend more time at work than on any other single activity. They probably spend more time with their colleagues than they do with their personal friends or possibly even their families. So, if they can't be themselves at work, that's a lot of time spent pretending.

Be yourself. Let them be themselves. And have fun together.

KEY POINTS

○ Fun at work is simply the freedom to be yourself at work. It's knowing that you are accepted for who you are and accepting your colleagues on the same terms.

○ Fun works because it's natural, not forced, and people find some of the best fun at work in routine day-to-day activities. Show your approval and just let it happen.

○ A high-trust, great place to work is a great place . . . *to work*. If an employee seems to be struggling to get the work-to-fun ratio right, don't hesitate to step in.

WHERE DO YOU GO FROM HERE?

TENS OF THOUSANDS OF GREAT managers around the world prove every day that the sixteen rules work for them. They'll work for you too. It happens subtly—a little more effort here and a little more thought there, a small tweak one day and a slightly different approach another. None of it is very noticeable until one day you just . . . emerge as a better you and a better manager, leading a better team. And, of course, a *happier* you leading a happier team. Happiness comes with the territory.

Here are some suggestions on how to manage your change:

REMEMBER YOUR NAME

You have two names. The name that you were given at birth, and the name that you make for yourself as you

journey through life. You will never have a better opportunity to make a name for yourself as a great, high-trust
manager. Go for it.

FIND WHAT WORKS FOR YOU

Think of the rules as inspiration. I've tried to focus on
ingredients rather than on recipes, with the intention
that you'll figure out the right way to combine them to
best effect. Find and adopt the rules that are the right
cultural fit for your team. If it doesn't feel right for your
team or for your organization, then it probably isn't a
good fit.

It's also important that the rules fit you as an individual. Don't try to adopt behaviors that, deep down, you
know don't suit your personality or work style. I'm not
suggesting that you don't need to change anything, but
you can only be a great manager if you feel comfortable
in your own skin and in your job. You can only make
your team comfortable and accepted if *you* feel comfortable and able to be yourself.

CREATE A "STOP-START-CONTINUE" PLAN

Read through the sixteen rules again, and when something resonates with you, jot it down on one of three lists:

- Stop: If an aspect of your behavior is at odds with what the best managers do, or if what you're doing just isn't working, consider stopping this.

- Start: When you're inspired to change an existing behavior or try a new idea or initiative, include it on this list of things that you want to start doing (or start doing differently).

- Continue: When you read a rule and realize that you're happy with what you do in this area, or you recognize something that is working well now, add it to the list of things that you should keep on doing.

These lists will be the foundation of your action plan, which, like any great plan, you will review periodically and change as needed. Be sure to fully document the positive behaviors and attitudes that belong on your "continue" list—you'll need this list to remind yourself of your many strengths when you suffer setbacks or become discouraged, as you inevitably will. Be fair to yourself, and make sure that this list fully reflects what you do well.

THINK BIG BUT START SMALL

Please, don't try to effect a personality change! First, it's not necessary—your current behaviors and actions need fine-tuning, not a complete overhaul. Second, people don't like change—even change that might ultimately benefit them—if that change is too drastic, unexpected, or unexplained. Apart from unnerving the people around you, big changes are very difficult to sustain over a prolonged period. Such change tends to fizzle out as quickly as it started—just think about New Year's resolutions!

Instead, pick one thing from your list and do it well. Focus your efforts exclusively on that. As a rule of thumb, it takes thirty days to make a habit, thirty days to break a habit. So, try a twelve-stage plan spread over a year, with each stage lasting one month and focusing on one goal—a single element that you want to either stop, start, or change. And if at any stage you suffer a setback or feel overwhelmed, turn to your "continue" list as a reminder of all the things that you already do brilliantly.

PLAN MONTHLY, VISUALIZE DAILY

Write down this month's goal. Describe exactly how you plan to behave, and how you and others will benefit. It might read:

"Goal: I will be a better listener. How: I will speak less and listen more. I will give my full attention, keep good eye contact, and show that I am listening. Benefits: I will understand my team better and they will know that I value and appreciate their views and opinions."

Take a few minutes every day to read it. Have it pop up on your phone or computer as a reminder a few times during the day. Or go low-tech with strategically placed Post-it notes. But be discreet—you don't want others to see these notes. Your reminder might be a single-word prompt to remind you of the full written goal. For example, if you're working on the listening goal above, your prompt could be "Listen" or maybe the more cryptic "2:1," a reminder that you have two ears and one mouth and that you should remember to use them in that proportion.

REFLECT DAILY

Set aside five minutes at some point each day to reflect on your progress toward high-trust management. If possible, aim for the same time each day—for example, early morning or on your evening commute—so that it becomes part of your normal routine. If you're working on changing a specific behavior, ask yourself, "How did I do? Successes? Any failures? Do I need to tweak my approach? Is my initiative affecting my team? How do I know? Do they seem happier? Are they getting more done and producing quality work? And how is it affecting me? Am I happier? Walking taller? And if not, why not?"

KEEP A DIARY
—

If you're going to take the time to plan, visualize, and reflect, why not go the whole hog and keep a diary? Jot down your successes and failures, along with your thoughts on why and how things went so well . . . or so badly. You'll find this a fascinating record of your journey to high-trust management and a source of encouragement when you're stuck, as you sometimes will be.

SEEK SUPPORT
—

Change can be tough. Some of us like to battle alone; others prefer a listening ear and an encouraging word. Would you benefit from sharing your plans with a trusted colleague or friend? If you have a mentor—formal or otherwise—consider sharing your "stop-start-continue" lists with them and asking for their honest feedback.

When the going gets tough, they'll remind you why you are doing this, and their support and encouragement will be invaluable as you do the hard work of adopting new habits and behaviors.

HAVE PATIENCE

Just because you change something doesn't mean that everyone else will. If your team is not accustomed to your asking about their lives outside of work, you can't expect them to give you chapter and verse the first time that you ask what they did over the weekend. Or if you've never really asked employees for their suggestions on job-related matters, don't be surprised if they take a while to open up. But stick with it. You're playing for the big prize.

IT'S WHY, NOT WHAT

What matters most to your people is not *what* you do for them, but *why* you do it. It's not really the surprise Monday-morning doughnuts that they appreciate, but that you care enough to stop off on your morning commute to buy them. Just a reminder.

EVERY MANAGER CAN BE A GREAT MANAGER

I opened this book with a simple statement: managers matter. You now know what the world's best managers do that others don't, and you know why they do it. Join them. You can be a great, high-trust manager. It's your time.

RECOMMENDED READING

The Great Workplace: How to Build It, How to Keep It, and Why It Matters, by Michael Burchell and Jennifer Robin

The Speed of Trust: The One Thing That Changes Everything, by Stephen M. R. Covey

The Trustworthy Leader: Leveraging the Power of Trust to Transform Your Organization, by Amy Lyman

No Excuses: How You Can Turn Any Workplace into a Great One, by Jennifer Robin and Michael Burchell

Make Their Day! Employee Recognition That Works, by Cindy Ventrice

The Decision to Trust: How Leaders Create High-Trust Organizations, by Robert F. Hurley

ACKNOWLEDGMENTS

L ET'S START AT THE VERY beginning. I want to thank Robert Levering for his pioneering research into how and why the world's best workplaces do what they do. Robert realized early on that every organization could become a great place to work, and he has dedicated much of his working life to spreading that message, even when it was neither popular nor profitable to do so.

I have been fortunate to work with some truly inspirational leaders at Great Place to Work Institute and I am particularly grateful to Jose Tolovi Jr. for his encouragement when this book was just the seed of an idea, and to Ann Nadeau for helping to keep the idea alive when challenges arose. Thanks also to Michael Bush for articulating a vision of a Great Place to Work for All— one in which ALL people are inspired to achieve their full human potential. Your insights provided clarity and direction when I lost focus or strayed off course.

Thank you to my many fantastic Great Place to Work colleagues around the world for your enthusiasm and total dedication to our mission of making a better world, one workplace at a time. Thanks also for your wisdom and advice, your support, and your friendship. Especially your friendship.

Thank you to the countless managers, employees, and organizations worldwide that have shared their experiences, opinions, and insights over the years, creating the opportunity for me to more fully understand the impact of trust in the workplace. Without you, this book would not exist!

It takes a lot more work and attention to detail to bring a book to fruition than I ever imagined. I am grateful for the encouragement, support, and direction of Genoveva Llosa, and to the fantastic team at Girl Friday Productions, including Paul Barrett for his superb design work, and, especially, Karen Upson for cheerfully and efficiently bringing it all together. Thanks also to Giselle Chacon Nessi for her keen design eye and invaluable advice.

I am grateful to my late father, Paschal, for encouraging my curiosity, and to my mother, Ann Lee, for fueling my love of reading and an obsessive appreciation of the importance of a correctly placed apostrophe. Thanks to my children, Kathy, Stephen, Lily, and Maria, for being my number-one fans while at the same time keeping my feet planted firmly on the ground.

Most of all, thanks to my wife and best friend, Eileen Devlin, for your unwavering support, endless patience, and always-honest feedback. More than ever, the world needs truth tellers.

Finally, thank *you*. If you've read through the acknowledgements this far, there's a very strong chance that you came to this page hoping to see your name here. I'm sorry—in the rush to meet the publication deadline, I forgot to mention you! Please accept my sincere apologies for the oversight, and my sincere thanks for your contribution! We both know that I couldn't have done it without you.

SOURCES

A NOTE ON THE SURVEY DATA and findings behind *Trust Rules*:

The sixteen rules are based on responses from nearly two million employees in eighty countries worldwide to the Great Place to Work® Trust Index© Survey.

The Trust Index© is the starting point for organizations committed to building a better workplace. It is one of the most widely used employee surveys in the world, used by over 6,000 organizations each year representing the views and experiences of approximately twelve million employees.

Please see trustrules.com for further information.

ENDNOTES

1. Robert Levering, "The Great Place to Work® Trust Model," https://www.youtube.com/user/GreatPlaceToWorkInc.

2. Robert Levering, *A Great Place to Work* (Great Place to Work Institute, 2000), 26.

3. Visit trustrules.com for full information on these and other studies along with the latest analysis and insights.

4. Alex Edmans, "Does the Stock Market Fully Value Intangibles? Employee satisfaction and equity prices," http://faculty.london. edu/aedmans/Rowe.pdf, doi:10.1016/j.jfineco.2011.03.021; "The link between job satisfaction and firm value, with implications for corporate social responsibility," Academy of Management Perspectives 26:4 (2012): 1–19.

5. Alex Edmans, "The social responsibility of business," TEDx talk, TEDx London Business School, https://youtu.be/Z5KZh-m19EO0.

6. Ibid.

7. Robert F. Hurley, "The Decision to Trust," Harvard Business Review (September 2006): 55–62. HBR Reprint Reference R0609B.

8. Thomas Barta, Markus Kleiner, and Tilo Neumann, "Is There a Payoff from Top-Team Diversity?", http://www.mckinsey.com/ business-functions/organization/our-insights/is-there-a-pay-off-from-top-team-diversity.

9. Jeff Shore, "Have You Mastered the 3 Rules of Talk:Listen Ratio?", http://jeffshore.com/2015/03/the-talk-listen-ratio-for-sales/.

10. Alan G. Robinson & Dean M. Schroeder, *The Idea-Driven Organization: Unlocking the Power in Bottom-Up Ideas* (Berrett-Koehler Publishers, 2014), xi.

11. Cindy Ventrice, *Make Their Day! Employee Recognition That Works* (Berrett-Koehler Publishers, 2009), 189.

12. Vivian Giang, "71% Of Millennials Want Their Co-Workers To Be A 'Second Family,'" Business Insider (June 15, 2013), http:// www.businessinsider.com/millennials-want-to-be-connected-to-their-coworkers-2013-6?IR=T.

NOTES

ABOUT THE AUTHOR

BOB LEE IS AN INTERNATIONALLY recognized conference speaker and media commentator and a senior leader for Great Place to Work—the global authority on high-trust, high-performance workplace cultures.

Bob has represented Great Place to Work at conferences and events all over the world, sharing his unique insights on how and why the world's best employers use great workplace culture to drive competitive advantage.

A founding director of Great Place to Work UK and Ireland, Bob held senior leadership positions with the institute, including four years as chair of its Global Advisory Board. He continues to support global multinational clients in his role as a lead consultant with Great Place to Work USA. Bob holds an MBA from the University College Dublin Smurfit Business School. *Trust Rules* is his first book.

CPSIA information can be obtained
at www.ICGtesting.com
Printed in the USA
LVHW021452080219
606907LV00017B/793/P

9 780995 737891